Job Out
'Probationer'
(The first Y(

by Me Fairn

One fire burns out another's burning
One pain is lessened by another's anguish...
Romeo & Juliet

Chapter 1

Siren wailing and the metallic clang of its bell, our 1953 Rolls Royce, Dennis F 8 Pump, screamed flat out in second gear as we turned into Washburn Street. Confronted by clouds of black putrid smoke billowing from shattered first floor windows, this was my first experience of a large city-centre fire as a Probationary Fireman.

I was nearly twenty and I lived with my mother in a small rented back-to-back, part furnished terraced house. A month before I was born Mother scrambled for safety from a war-torn Germany. Arriving at last in England, she suffered from several abusive attacks, having to uproot us and move home several times. Eventually we settled in Torridge City, a city with a population of nearly half a million people where we struggled to be accepted.

My school days were hard and difficult. Money was always short and so Mother took all kinds of jobs to make ends meet washing, cleaning, working evenings in the local off licence shop. At school I struggled with all forms of theory, especially arithmetic, and cruel childish racial taunts taught me to trust no one.

Leaving school as early as possible I tried several jobs until Mother, in her guttural English, read out an advertisement one evening from the local paper which said, 'young men wanted to join Torridge City Fire Service'.

"Sicherheit and a pensionable future," she told me.

Security and pension at my age? I would be twenty in a few months; the very thought of a pensionable salary was of no interest to me. But as winter approached, the thought of continuing to work in cold damp buildings, churning out never-ending mountains of wet plaster for an ever hungry and demanding craftsman made the thought of another change welcome. I was an inch short of the specified five feet eight inches but even so I posted a letter for an application form.

A reply to my letter arrived, telling me to attend an appointment with the Police Surgeon for an examination at Torridge City Town Hall. This included a brief medical interview with a doctor. My chest was sounded by stabs from the freezing end of a stethoscope; I quickly looked through a thick and well-thumbed book with numbers hidden amidst dots of different colours and finally answered questions about an eye chart hung at a crazy angle on the back of a door.

At half-past nine in the morning, four days later, I walked with some trepidation into the headquarters of Torridge City Fire Brigade. I was wearing my best and only suit. I was about to take the entrance exam.

My dark green suit had been purchased second-hand, its trousers shortened by my mother. It showed polished crease marks pointing forwards, a result of constant steam pressing. The winter was cold, very cold, turning to be one of the coldest on record.

Divisional Officer Chad, tall and gaunt, was in full uniform, complete with a very impressive cap which displayed a white silver band on the peak. He introduced himself. His jacket, he explained was known in the Fire Brigade as the undress uniform. As a Divisional Officer he was entitled to wear rank markings, consisting of a large impeller, like a miniature pyramid encircled by a laurel wreath, fashioned in shiny metal and standing erect and proud as they rested snugly on his shoulders.

His cap, pressed firmly on his head, and had a half-inch of silver braid on the peak.

"An impeller is a miniature copy of the internal workings of our water pumps," he explained.

He removed his cap, leaving a red ring indented under his grey hair. From a piece of paper, he proceeded to call out our names. He swung his pencil like a baton as if he were a conductor.

"Stephen Saury?" Dipping his pencil in acknowledgement of the answering.

"Yes Sir," Stephen answered.

"Michael Edward Fairn? Yes," I answered.

I stepped forward to stand alongside Stephen Saury. (Mother had altered our surnames in her attempt to prevent any recurrences of racial problems.)

"Yes, Sir," Divisional Officer Chad gave his instruction shouting as though I were deaf.

Out of the six names the Divisional Officer called out, one man had not bothered to turn up and as the remaining five of us answered, he ticked off our names with an emphatic swing of his pencil.

Then we were ushered into a long thin room with a row of desks arranged in neat lines.

"Just a few measurements to check your application form," said a stumpy man with a squeaky voice. He was dressed in a brown pin-striped suit and like mine had obviously seen better days. A dirty white tape measure hung around his neck.

"Follow me! Stand against the wall," he squeaked.

As each of us stood against the wall, the man held a ruler on the top of our heads and stretched to his full height before marking the wall surface behind us with a small stub of chalk.

When my turn came I could not help noticing the heavy odour of tobacco oozing from his clothes. Unaware of the stench he carried, he held the ruler in a level position as I moved away.

"You aren't tall enough," he informed me.

"You should be five-feet and eight-inches! You're an inch short." My heart sank.

"You'll have to try again." His voice went up an octave. Once more taking a deep breath, I stood against the wall.

"Stand up a bit, on your toes."

Gaining an extra inch or so in this way I achieved the minimum height required.

"Now your chest measurements."

Almost as quickly as the tape measure went around my chest the necessary two-inch expansion was accepted.

"You'll do. Next."

After each of us had quickly gone through this charade, we were told to sit at the desks. We were given a clean piece of white lined paper and the Divisional Officer began asking general knowledge questions. He pulled an old crumpled exercise book from one of his uniform pockets and began.

"Name of the Prime Minister? Longest river in the world? Capital of Egypt?"

The questions came fast. We scribbled down our answers. More followed. My page slowly filled. Papers handed in for marking we were then ushered outside into a cold and icy morning for the practical side of the entrance examination. Two on-duty firemen waited impatiently to demonstrate the requirements to potential recruits. One of the firemen, a huge chap in pale-blue overalls, which were more, washed out than true blue, picked up the second fireman like a rag doll. He bounced the fireman across his shoulders and proceeded to amble casually up the back street just as if he was carrying nothing at all. He walked twenty yards or so turned and trotted back before dropping the fireman from his broad shoulders to the ground. His warm breath shot out from his mouth, blanketing his face in clouds of steam.

"Pick a mate!" Divisional Officer Chad instructed. Dutifully we paired off. I looked for a partner I thought I could lift.

"Right get on with it. Let's not be shy."

From the officer's manner it appeared that we did not have a great deal of time. I looked carefully at my opponent. He looked about my size. Thrusting my right arm around his waist, I made him lean forward and bend down slightly from his hips. I managed to support the man across my shoulders and as I straightened myself it not only felt uncomfortable but also top heavy. It's easier carrying bags of plaster, I thought. Perhaps there was a special technique carrying a live body? Unsteadily I trod carefully up the street, turned and with my legs shaking hurried back and deposited my partner eagerly on the ground.

"Next!"

Another couple went through the same procedure.

"Go a bit further," Divisional Office Chad shouted as this pair turned, trying to shorten the distance.

When it came to my turn, to be carried, I felt distinctly odd, upside down and across someone else' shoulders.

A ladder appeared, and the two firemen demonstrated our next task. Placing the ladder against a wall, one held the base securely as the other climbed about fifteen feet up. He put one leg through the ladder rungs and, using just his leg to grip, he let go with his hands and leant outwards.

"This is a leg lock," the Divisional Officer told us, "so we can tell if any of you are frightened of heights."

The first applicant to stand at the bottom gripped the sides of the ladder. He was stopped immediately.

"Rest!" the Divisional Officer, shouted.

"In the Fire Brigade we hold on to the rounds, you'll no doubt think of them as rungs. The sides of the ladder are known as strings."

The big fireman stepped forward and began another demonstration.

"Use your left hand, left foot, right hand, right foot." He began to scale the ladder. It looked so easy.

I felt confident and volunteered to be next. Used to climbing ladders on building sites, I too climbed the ladder as if I was carrying a hod of ready mixed plaster gripping both sides of the ladder. But this was not what was taught in the Fire Service.

"You a window cleaner?" the big Fireman grunted.

"Window cleaners do not use rounds because of getting muck on their shoes," he told me.

"But they are not likely to carry anything other than their shammy-leather," he continued.

"At all times a round, or in your words a rung, must be gripped in one hand."

He could not resist showing again his talent for climbing as he climbed the ladder once more. But on his way down he deliberately slipped and fell. His feet fell away but he hung with one hand quite securely. He had proved his point.

With the practical examinations completed, five of us were sent in the direction of the canteen for much needed refreshments. They were welcome after the bitter cold temperatures outside.

The Police Fire Brigade originally used Torridge City Fire Station, a hotchpotch of buildings. Built at the end of the nineteenth century, through the decades an assortment of dwellings gave the place a higgledy-piggledy untidy appearance with the ancient Police Headquarters now converted into the main office block. The large four bay engine house was adapted from the horse drawn steam pump era to accommodate today's petrol driven appliances.

The canteen, to be found up a flight of well-worn stone stairs, looked like a church hall. Its high ceiling, its large wooden beams and its stone floor did nothing to reduce the bitter cold of the day. In one corner a Radio Rental speaker, played apparently to itself. Sounds of a new group of musicians and the words 'love me do' blasted out into the room.

"Come for a drink of tea?" A voice carried over the music from a small hatch cut into the far wall. Nervously the five of us crept towards the questioner, to be confronted by a small dainty woman wearing a large white coat that fell to within an inch off the floor. Her hair was draped in a bright red and yellow flowered patterned scarf.

"And something to eat?" she asked. Coming from inside her kitchen and screwing her hands tightly through a white towel, she went to turn down the Beatles.

"Maurice always has this thing on too loud. Then he goes out, leaving it blaring away. I'm Blanche Spurling. Now lads, what do you want?"

She shuffled back into her kitchen. Her long white coat brushed the floor as she walked.

"Bread and dripping!" called a voice from somewhere inside our group.

She stood alongside a large copper water heater, straining up to reach the handle. Boiling water spluttered out from the spout into a large aluminium teapot. Clouds of steam danced upwards.

"Come to join the Fire Brigade, have you?" Blanche Spurling asked, as the teapot slowly filled. She plonked it onto an enamel tray, which held a bowl of sugar. Five white plastic mugs followed in quick succession before she lifted the tray in both hands. We followed her sheepishly to a table. Without further ado she was back in her kitchen and, reaching for a large knife, proceeded to cut into a loaf of bread.

"Sit down, don't just stand about!" she ordered.

We each nervously selected a chair. Through the door a man wearing a brown overall coat entered.

"Maurice?" the canteen lady greeted him, "some new recruits."

Maurice never said a word. He went over to the Radio Rental speaker and, twisting the volume knob, filled the room once more with loud music.

Carrying a large plate stacked high with slices of bread three quarters of an inch thick and plastered in dark beef dripping, Blanche Spurling sat down with us, her feet dangling under the chair. Treating us as if she were a mother hen she began.

"Before you finish this morning, providing you have all passed, Chief will want to see you. He'll ask, "Why do you want to join? Whatever you think," she went on, "don't say it's for the money! Alan Bass, the Chief, doesn't like to think men join just for the money. I have known him for many years, since well before the war began. Now he's Chief, and he still speaks to me!" She clucked on at us.

She commanded our attention, going through our expected interview step by step.

Divisional Officer Chad returned to collect us after we had eagerly devoured Blanche's full plate of dripping sandwiches and had downed her mugs of sweet tea. Blanche rose, from her chair, collected our empty plates and cups and went off into her kitchen.

"All five have passed the entrance examination," Divisional Officer Chad said in a dull uninterested tone.

"One or two of you need to brush up on your general knowledge. Harold Macmillan is the Prime Minister. And the capital of Egypt is Cairo," a sly smile cracked his face into two.

"Not to worry," he added, "you can all read and write. Now the Chief and the Assistant Chief need to interview you all before you are accepted," he told us as we followed him out of the canteen.

Five of us followed the officer back down the stone stairs and along a corridor to a new and as yet unseen section of the headquarters.

"Wait here," he said.

We stood outside a large brown polished door as he tapped gently on it and entered. The door did not have time to close before it sprung wide open again and the first of us was asked inside. As the rest of us were left idle, standing outside, I attempted to make casual conversation. But before I could exchange anything more than the day's cold weather, the large door opened and we were told to make less noise.

This is just like the hours spent outside the headmaster's study in my school days, I whispered to myself.

The interviews lasted only a few moments and since our names were taken in alphabetical order I did not have long to wait before the call came for Fairn. I entered through the big door. The room looked dark and sombre. Chief Officer Bass sat behind a large leather topped-desk. His uniform looked impressive with masses of silver buttons and markings of rank.

Two red lines pointed downwards on his lapels. Alongside him another Officer sat dressed similar. To his left sat a civilian in a brown suit.

He was the man smelling of tobacco we had met earlier when he had been taking our measurements. Behind the three men a hot blazing fire glowed from a huge fireplace, sending waves of comfort into the room.

"So, you want to be a fireman?" The Chief's words were brief and clipped.

"Why?"

I thought of the canteen lady, Mrs Spurling.

"The job offers security," I answered.

"Not the money?" the Chief turned to the Officer at his side. "Blanche must have been giving advice," he muttered. Obviously, a man of few words, he sat back in his chair, leaving the other officer to continue the interview.

"My name is Richard Albert Carp, Assistant Chief Officer. This is Mr Parr the Brigade clerk," he began.

"Just a few questions about you," he spoke quickly.

"How old are you, laddie?"

"Nineteen," I answered.

"Now laddie, when are you going to be twenty?"

"April this year. Sir. The twentieth," I added as an afterthought.

"You start at 9 o'clock next Friday morning."

Chapter 2

Beginning work on a Friday is different to being in the outside world. Most work places finish their week on a Friday, or Saturday; for some obscure reason Torridge City Fire Brigade begins its week on a Friday!

"So, you were ill with sickness and diarrhoea?" the owner of the plastering firm where I had been working said with malice in his voice, "so how come we received a letter from the local Fire Brigade today wanting references?"

The Torridge City Fire Brigade had sent a letter to the firm I was working for.

"So 'Kraut' wants to join the 'Feuerwehr'?" The owner mimicked what he thought was a German accent, displaying a prejudice no doubt derived from his war service.

"You can finish now. Today," he added.

My employment terminated immediately. I collected my bundle of old working clothes from the workshed and my old pedal cycle, fetching it from the array of cycles under a corrugated shed. I pedalled home slowly feeling harassed and dejected and short of four day's pay.

Mother was shocked at my sudden appearance. A smile darted for a fleeting second across her well-worn creased face and revealed her inward pleasure for a second before she composed herself. The smell of bleach drifted from her hands and wafted after her as she darted off to the scullery and proceeded to rattle a few pots in the sink.

I removed my thick duffel coat and moved closer to the fire, where a few embers struggled for life. Mother had deliberately allowed the morning fire to die in an effort to save fuel. The times were hard and my new appointment as a fireman with a weekly starting wage of eleven pounds and one penny would mean a further loss; I was earning £14, and sometimes £15 a week mixing plaster.

"You need a job with a pension," mother shouted from her kitchen.

Pension, I thought! Who thinks of a pension at twenty years of age?

On Friday, still dressed in civilian clothes, I arrived back at Torridge City Fire Station ready to begin my new life. Dressed for a keen frosty morning, with two thick woollen jumpers covered by my working duffel coat, I leaned my Old Faithful bicycle against a wall.

"You can't park that there!" The voice boomed with authority as I meekly whispered an apology.

"You new?" The voice went on.

"Park that thing over there," he ordered. I moved the bicycle obediently.

"Please can you tell me where to go?" I aimed my question at the voice giving all the orders. But the Fireman in uniform simply turned and walked away without answering my question.

Another fireman, tall thin and smart, intervened. Even the sleeves of his black uniform jacket supported straight creases and the peak of his hat was polished to look like glass; it reflected the view.

"Come this way, kid, take no notice of the old moaner. He's always grumpy after being on nights. My name is Norman Sterlet and I'm a Union official. We've just finished a fifteen-hour night and we're ready to go off duty now. The day crew will look after you," Norman Sterlet told the other newcomers and me. I joined the other familiar faces from the previous week's interview. We all looked nervous, overawed by the number of men jostling about. At nine o'clock the Station changed shifts from night to day crew. Both crews

11

assembled and formed up in two lines. We stood and watched as the morning parade began.

"Parade 'Shun!" Someone shouted.

Two rows of firemen straightened, standing to attention.

"Off-going watch is dismissed."

Turning smartly to the right, a group of Firemen walked away.

"On-coming watch stand at ease. Red watch answer your names."

It all seemed very efficient, if rather alarming.

The Station Officer in charge of the Red Watch day crew, dressed in a white shirt with two chrome impellers on the shoulders of his uniform jacket, introduced himself and told a Leading Fireman to look after our needs.

"Follow me to the stores," he said.

Deposited at the entrance to the stores, we were greeted by a white-haired gentleman wearing a grey-white coat, not dirty but washed until it was grey; his hair looked whiter than his coat. A man of few words, he whistled continuously; it was not a particular melody but just a constant drone up and down the musical scale. As he whistled, notes from his mouth steamed out in narrow tubes as his warm breath hit the cold air. He unlocked a door, using a large key on a chain fastened underneath his coat. We followed him inside where, lit by a single light bulb hung from the centre of the ceiling, the stores-man laid a sheet of paper carefully onto a table top.

"Who's Fairn?" Was his first utterance as he read from the list of names on his paper.

"This will be your pile of clothes."

"Who is Saury?" He went down the list, calling out our names. We all stood obediently alongside our allotted places as he kept disappearing to the shelves and returning with armfuls of clothing. The piles of kit on the table grew and grew.

"Try these for size." He first looked, made a guess handed us what he thought would fit. We ended up with

An old fire-helmet.
A new leather belt, pouch and fireman's axe.
Two new pairs of serge fire-trousers.
Two fire-tunics, both second hand.
A new pair of leather fire-boots.
A pair of used leather fire-boots.
Two new pairs of socks.
Two new shirts with detached collars.
A new black tie.
New set of overalls.
A second-hand undress jacket.
A new uniform cap.
One new pair of undress trousers.
Two new pairs of shoes.
Two new pairs of grey woollen socks.
A new pillow.
Three new grey woollen blankets.
One gas mask complete with canvas shoulder bag.

"No raincoats, old greatcoats will have to do," he muttered as he folded our thick black, uniform greatcoats on the floor in front of us.

"No underwear?" the ginger-haired Stephen Saury enquired.

The stores man heard him. He looked at Saury and momentarily stopped whistling, but said nothing. Choosing to ignore the question, he carried on, pursing his lips and continuing to whistle the tuneless melody.

"No underwear?" Repeated Stephen Saury, not prepared to have his question left unanswered. His freckled face pleaded for an answer.

"The Army supplied everything, even vests and underpants," he added. But there was no acknowledgement. The shrill whistle just continued without interruption.

The uniform cap, shirts, tie, socks, shoes, pillow, blankets and fire-boots all looked new but the rest of the equipment seemed to be second hand.

The fire-helmets had definitely been used before. Made of leather, they resembled the helmet Britannia wore on a penny piece. A large curved pinnacle protruded and arched over the top and obviously a World War One issue. The gas masks in its canvas bag were supplied for the next World War and the threat of nuclear fall out.

"Fire-helmets are expensive," the stores man told us.

"You'll get a proper one if you stay the distance." A few brief words had at last interrupted his tuneless drone.

The Leading Fireman, the first rank after a promotion, returned and took us to what he called the hose room. We felt like heavily burdened packhorses. We climbed up a long steep staircase before entering a low ceiling room lined with racks full of lengths of hose. "After your had dinner, all this equipment needs marking with your number," he told us.

It was midday already. The morning had already disappeared. Following the Leading Fireman through an array of stairs, alleyways, passageway, and yet more stairs, we eventually arrived at the canteen which looked like a church hall. The day watch duty crew sat, already eating and the room briefly hushed as we entered.

Blanche Spurling, the petite canteen lady, greeted us with the motherly affection she had shown at our first meeting week earlier.

"You'll want something warm to eat?" She asked. Her fresh stiff white coat circled her like a white tube.

"It's fish and chips. Always fish and chips on Fridays." Her strong positive manner belied her small frame. It did not seem possible one so small could speak so firmly. She produced five dinners, which she had already prepared.

Large white plates, with a huge piece of fried cod surrounded by dozens of finger thick chips, appeared from her kitchen. A dollop of mushy peas, ladled over the tail end of the fish, sat motionless like green wet concrete. The plate felt heavy as we carried off our dinners and found places to sit and eat. Rice pudding followed the fish, looking like the mushy peas, only white!

"Enjoy that?" Blanche enquired as she collected the empty plates; their emptiness answered her question.

We followed the Leading Fireman and the rest of the duty crew, and were introduced to the recreation area. The Leading Fireman explained, almost lovingly, the history of the Fire Station. We sat around him and digested every word. Built in the 1880s, he began; this Fire Station grew through two world wars from the old horse-drawn era of a Police City Fire Brigade to the present day.

We sat in the long-room. This was the area where firemen spent their leisure stand-down time. All four walls were covered by frescoes, showing the marvels of the world; Chinese Geisha girls, Paris, Venice, and the Great Pyramids had all originally been designed and painted by an artistic fireman. In the middle of one of the long walls was an enormous fireplace. There was no shortage of fuel here. The heat from the fire was immediately noticeable as the warmth struck our cheeks. The massive red-hot glowing coke-fired grate blasted hundreds of therms into the room. Its welcome was overpowering.

Dinner hour ended, and it was a real effort to move after such a large meal and after half an hour under the spell of a furnace. But the cold air outside cruelly brought us to reality as we gathered for the marking and numbering of the kit issue from the morning.

Each of us was presented with our Brigade number, which was to be our identification for the rest of our service in Torridge City Fire Brigade. Using a well-used stencil, I duly labelled every item. 'M.E.FAIRN, T.C.F.B. C435' the white painted lettering eventually adorned every article of my uniform. We obediently stamped metal and leather objects, axe, belt buckle, boots with steel punches.

"What is the C for?" I asked sheepishly.

The Leading Fireman looked straight at me but said nothing. Remaining mute in answer to questions seemed endemic.

Cold grey daylight turned to pitch darkness as home time arrived.

"Take home with you a shirt, tie, trousers, shoes, and socks and report tomorrow, Saturday dressed in uniform." This order was the Leading Fireman's final word.

Struggling with my brown paper parcel precariously balanced on the crossbar, I pedalled home.

"Been to any fires yet?" Mother asked in her guttural accent.

I sat down for tea. Mother produced a plate of fish and chips. Always fish on Fridays, she had learnt, an English custom. I was keen and excited about my new job. There was so much to tell; Mother listened interestedly as my second fish dinner that day vanished.

On the following morning, Saturday, I struggled to fit the detachable collar to the blue shirt. Stiff as plywood, even with proper collar studs, produced magically by my mother the separate collar did not like the idea of living on a shirt.

Worrying about being late for duty I left home to collect my old push-bike normally that was kept twenty yards down the street in our outside toilets. But there was no bicycle. It had gone, stolen during the night. There was nothing to do but to walk and run to the Fire Station. My new uniform felt strange and uncomfortable. The new shoes pinched, the undress jacket was too big, the cap was too small and the uniform trousers needed a pair of braces to hold them in place.

"No cap-badge in your hat," an officer shouted at me. Met by yet another Station Officer, the change of watches took place and a new crew began on duty. The officers wore a uniform that was different from that of the firemen; it was tailored with outside pockets and a small material belt with a gleaming buckle, which sparkled, from the front.

None of us five recruits had been given cap-badges. This was another expensive item to be issued later.

Saturday morning was packed with more indoctrination, this time from another Leading Fireman who introduced himself as Geoffrey Sardelle. He explained his family had connections with Torridge City Fire Brigade going back for many years. His Grandfather, who served at the beginning of the century, had worked in the Brigade when horses drew fire-pumps. He went on to say that in those days' firemen worked almost a continuous duty and the average turn-out times for horse-drawn pumps, fully equipped, was fifty seconds by day and seventy seconds by night.

In those days they all lived in houses built around the Station, each house having its own alarm bell. Many of these houses still existed and were still used by Firemen and their families. Today they provided cheap handy accommodation. Like his father before him, Geoffrey Sardelle was born in one of these houses. His father, who worked when Fire Brigades throughout the country were amalgamated in 1941, forming a National Fire Service during the Second World War, was a victim of an enemy bombing raid after being mobilised from Torridge City to cover the blitz on the dock land areas suffering fatal injuries. I grimaced at mention of a German enemy, chewed my inner lip, and said nothing.

His knowledge of and insight into the present-day Fire Service was full of depth and personal feeling; he spoke about it with such pride and cherished memories. He explained that there were three shifts, or watches, known as Red, White and Blue. One of the colours was on duty 0900 to 1800 hours. The second watch worked nights from 1800 to the following morning at 0900 hours, a total of fifteen hours on nights! The third shift enjoyed rota leave and had three days off duty. Every three days the system changed; the watch working days went onto nights, the night crew went onto rota leave and the crew off duty began their three days on. The long nights with fifteen-hours on duty began after the introduction of shorter working hours. It was considered important to have Firemen available and working through the night for continuity. Many fires occurred during the night and changing crews over in mid-shift was considered impracticable. Because of these long nights, firemen were allowed to sleep in the Station; it was cheaper to keep men in bed than to keep them occupied and awake subject to immediate turnout by the station alarm bells. Geoffrey Sardelle explained turnout times on nights were faster than those in the day. Sleeping times, called 'boots off', lasted between the hours of midnight and reveille at 0645 hours.

The long duty periods that Geoffrey Sardelle's predecessors endured created many hours not regarded as working time but still kept the men confined on station and ready for fire-calls. Sundays, Saturday afternoons, evenings, and any bank holidays were considered stand-down periods, times when station-working routines were relaxed.

Down the years, these stand-down periods were often filled by recreation pastimes. Ball games, football, cricket, and a crude form of tennis were all played outside, on the back street. A licensed bar provided drinks and a social get-together during the leisure periods, though the bar was now restricted to an hour on night shift and to the midday breaks on Saturday and Sundays.

By the time Geoffrey had completed his historic account it was midday and we had reached the end of our day and a half induction. His offer to stay and have a drink at the bar was most welcome; pint of mild beer went down well. The white creamy froth clung to the sides of the pint glass as the dark brown nectar quenched our avid thirst.

I had been given a glimpse of an entirely new world.

Chapter 3

Monday morning arrived. Rising in darkness before an idle January sun blessed the morning with its light, I struggled into my Fire Brigade uniform. The blue shirt with an attached stiff collar, bit deep into my neck. The black tie was fastened so tight I struggled to breathe. Uniform-trousers supported by a pair of braces hung like heavy curtains. New unbroken and pinching black shoes completed the cladding. I felt and looked like a stuffed dummy.

For a week, as five raw recruits, we received basic instruction. Every morning this consisted of handling ladders, running lengths of delivery hose, connecting the brass couplings and extending our hose-line up the backstreet of the Fire Station. Every afternoon we joined the duty crew and were introduced to the Station routines. Cleaning the Station occupied many hours as we waited for the station alarm bells to ring we were shown the 'mop and bucket'. I was soon to learn these items were to be a fireman's most important companion.

The following Monday a new shift, White Watch and Station Officer Finnan the officer in charge, began their three-day, three-night tour of duty.

Station Officer Finnan spoke with a marked Scottish accent. At first, I found it was difficult to understand him, but he seemed kind and reassuring. He explained that as recruits we could be posted to any of the five Fire Stations in Torridge City. We gathered in his office where he produced a piece of paper and sat down. The five of us shuffled around his desk, which was in a room six-foot square. He removed his cap, revealing black hair plastered down with hair cream and glistening under the electric light bulb. Down the centre of his head an immaculate parting divided his scalp exactly in half.

"Michael Edward Fairn is posted to this watch, Torridge City Station," he said to me.

The other four recruits were detailed to other Fire Stations dotted about the city. We trailed outside as all their equipment; blankets, helmets and fire-uniform were stuffed aboard a red Ford Thames van. The four recruits clambered in the back of the van with all their uniforms and blankets. The van sped off down the street as if turning out to a fire.

With his rank markings (two impellers sprouting from both shoulders all fashioned in shiny steel looking like four shiny nipples) Station Officer Finnan stood and watched the van as it left. The impellers, a design used in all officers' rank markings, consisted of a knurled steel knob, the size of a large button, with its central design imitating blades found inside Fire Service water-pumps.

"Thinks he's a racing driver! Tells me he wants to drive to fires." His words were quiet and more to himself than spoken out loud. Replacing his cap, he nodded for me to follow. I trailed close behind. The officer in charge of White Watch, Station Officer Finnan, possessed a kind and friendly face. He told me he controlled his men with kindness, respect and fairness and in return he demanded total commitment. Educated by life's experiences, his round plump face had the ability to express pleasure or annoyance by a single glance. I stood in front of his desk as he sat down. Removing his cap once again he carefully undid every chrome button on his jacket. Taking it off he draped it over the back of his chair. He sat down slowly to reveal an officer's white shirt, sectioned by maroon braces and split by a black tie. He began.

"A fireman's job can be compared to driving a nail into wood. Everyone seems to know the correct size, the type of nail and the correct type of hammer, even the proper trajectory and force needed. The manuals are full of this sort of theory, all perfectly true, but," he leaned across the table and looked at me closely, his face showing a hint of a smile, which quickly changed as he went on, "ultimately it needs someone to pick up the hammer and actually hit the nail!"

This brief introduction over, he called for Fireman Bleck to act as my mentor and protector for the next few days. Barry Bleck, tall, thin and wiry with tight curly red hair crowning his head, had eleven years service in the Fire Brigade.

"Get your fire-helmet, your axe, belt, boots, and tunic and I'll find you a peg." Barry told me.

Burdened down like a struggling packhorse I followed him into the muster-room. The muster-room was the hub of the Fire Station. It was a dimly lit room, even during daylight hours, the centre of operations and sited next to the engine house. On one wall was a crew-board, the size of a small window. Painted in red, white and blue, two sliding doors left the list of on-duty crew visible. Barry pointed to it. Down one side of the crew-board the titles of every fire-appliance on the Station were inscribed in black letters. Alongside every appliance was a line of small hooks and from these hooks hung small round steel discs, known as tallies! Each member of every watch had their own tally with their name written on it. Even the tallies were in the colour of the appropriate watch. I was impressed.

"This crew-board must be checked at all times," Barry Bleck standing alongside, fondling the tallies as he made his point.

"How we man the appliances rests on these names and when the bells sound it needs to be checked."

The tallies rattled and swung as his fingers brushed them. I looked at the numerous names, trying to commit some to memory.

WHITE WATCH

Pump One   *Stn.O. Finnan: Lfm.Loche: Fm.Tailor:*
Fm.Cale

Pump Escape   *Sub.O. Gardon: Fm.Scar: Fm.Bleck:*
Fm.Ronchil

Pump Two

Turntable Ladder *Fm.Twaite: Fm.Grundel*

Emergency Tender *Fm.Margot: Fm.Capelin*

Detached Duties *Fm.Partan*

Off Station   *Sub.O.Latchet: Lfm.Weever: Fm.Bley*
Fm.Dory Fm.Ray

Annual Leave *Fm.Kingstone*

Sick *Fm.Milter*

Named tallies hung against every title except Pump Two.

"Pump Two isn't usually manned during weekdays. There aren't enough men," Barry said.

Opposite the words 'Off Station' hung several tallies.

"These men are on duty but are off the Fire Station, working as tradesmen and doing repairs," Barry explained.

I learned that every watch should have a contingent of twenty-one men, when at full strength: Sixteen firemen, two Leading Firemen, two Sub-Officers and one Station Officer. With somebody always on holiday, or as they called it in the Fire Brigade 'annual leave', the number of men on duty should have averaged eighteen. But these numbers were rarely achieved.

The muster-room also housed everybody's fire-uniforms. Each member of the Station was allocated a peg on which he hung his fire-tunic. Above this peg on a shelf rested his fire-helmet, and below it, on another shelf, a pair of fire-boots were ready for collection the moment the bells sounded.

On another wall hung the indicator board listing the full compliment of appliances. When the alarm bells rang, lights behind this board showed which appliances were turning out. Men allocated to that machine collected their fire-uniform and went to the appliance.

"This will be your peg," Barry told me.

He placed the fire-helmet I had been issued on the shelf above the peg and my gas mask in its canvas bag on the peg. Over this he hooked my fire-tunic and then my axe on its leather belt. Carefully folding the fire-tunic around the belt, Barry formed a neat curled parcel. On the lower shelf, conveniently situated directly above some central heating pipes he placed my pair of leather fire-boots and told me.

"Because our uniforms are always on show, always make sure that your boots, your tunic, and your helmet are always left clean and tidy." My fire-uniform now hung neat and tidy alongside the rest of the Station's crews.

"Until you have a proper tally this will have to do," Barry said as he scribbled my name Fairn on an inch-square piece of cardboard and hooked it on one of the tiny hooks alongside the appliance named Pump One.

"But always check before we turn-out!"

I followed behind Barry as closely as possible. He bounced through a pair of swing doors to the engine house. I followed in hot pursuit. The line of fire-appliances I saw looked impressive; and they gleamed.

Two identical machines stood in the first two bays. They were early 1950s Dennis F8s with Rolls Royce engines and open-backed pumps. Each appliance carried a thirty-five-foot ladder, a hose-reel and eighty gallons of water. Barry opened the lockers to display the contents: rolls of delivery hose and specialised equipment in different lockers.

A Dennis F12 Pump Escape sat gleaming in the third bay. On its back there was a fifty-foot ladder. Above, the fully enclosed cab housed a ladder attached to two huge carriage wheels, which protruded from the rear. One of the two large wheels spun easily as Barry brushed the steel rim with his hand.

In the fourth bay was a 1955 Dennis F17 Turntable Ladder, again powered by a Rolls Royce petrol engine. A Turntable Ladder was a self-supporting mechanical hundred-foot ladder, I learned.

I was still only a foot behind Barry as we passed the Brigade Control Room door. This small insignificant door, Barry informed me, led into a secret room where all messages were received from the General Post Office. Strictly out of bounds to firemen, exclusively women manned Control. He whispered as he gave me this information.

Finally, he took me to the rear of the Station to show me an additional appliance, the Emergency Tender. I was very impressed by the large amount of specialised equipment carried on this appliance. Barry opened drawer after drawer and locker after locker, revealing all manner of equipment. The machine was packed tight with such things as spanners, cutting gear, breathing apparatus and emergency electric lighting. Barry told me that the Emergency Tender turned out to road accidents and any special incidents requiring this impressive array of equipment.

There was so much to digest it was probably a good thing the Station bells did not sound on my first full day!

Tuesday began as Monday had with morning parade and roll call. This time my name was actually called out on parade and I was detailed to ride on Pump Two. A freshly painted white tally was produced with my name Fm.Fairn. It hung neatly alongside the appropriate appliance on the crew-board.

Despite the severe frosty conditions, part of White Watch performed a drill outside, on the street at the back of the Station, which was used as the drill ground. The crew moved fast, leaning the ladder against the drill tower effortlessly. I could only stand, stare and once more be impressed.

Now the induction period was over I was re-introduced to the routine duties. One of these important tasks was for a fireman to heat the Fire Station. The fireman carrying out this particular duty was called 'The Yards and Fires Man' and I was detailed to seek out Fireman Brian Ronchil. His waist solid like a thick tree trunk, Brian gave me a guided tour of all the boilers dotted all over the Station. His task for the three days on duty was to keep these boilers producing heat and hot water for the whole station. Using large shovels, I assisted Brian as we thrust coke into the ever-open mouths of the many furnaces.

"Big Bernice is the biggest," Brian explained, "she supplies heat to the engine house and eats five tons of coke a week."

On Monday afternoon and on nearly the whole of Tuesday I continued to assist Brian coping with the demand from insatiable boilers. Still there was no sign of any turnout, but late on Tuesday afternoon, bells sounded at long last. This happened just as I was washing and getting ready to go home. With soap on my face I panicked and rushed out of the washroom and ran as fast as I could towards the muster-room.

The tinkling of one station alarm bell in the washroom had sounded like a bedside alarm clock. Outside, with several bells joining in, a cacophony of noise filled the night air as everybody on duty dashed forwards. Men appeared from all directions joining together as we banged through the well-bruised and polished entrance door into the muster-room.

25

In the rush I tried to locate my tally on the crew-board but with men coming in all directions, charging back and forth some collecting their fire-uniforms, I could not get close enough to see my name.

"Pump Two," someone cried.

"Grab your gear, you're on Pump Two," Barry Bleck shouted, finding me looking puzzled.

"Don't forget your helmet," someone else yelled.

I struggled, my arms full, through swing doors from the muster-room into the engine house. Pump Two had an open rear platform, which allowed us to climb on board easily. Our officer in charge, Sub Officer Gardon, collected his fire-message from a woman standing outside the Control Room. His fire-helmet was already on his head. (Sub Officer is one rank above a Leading Fireman and one rank below a Station Officer. Sub Officers had two chromium half-inch bars on their shoulders and their black fire-helmets displayed two red bands.)

The driver, Fireman Trevor Tailor, and the Sub Officer climbed aboard through their individual cab doors at the front. Their doors slammed shut.

Trevor was about forty. His blonde hair cut to no more than half an inch in length; cover his head like a field of standing corn. He brushed a hand constantly through this harvest in a repeated mannerism.

The engine roared into life. The engine house doors crashed open and in a second, we were rolling forwards. I held on tight. The single blue light turned slowly on the roof as we chased off.

I watched as the other two members of the crew got dressed. The helmets went on first, and then arms were thrust into tunics. Sitting on the polished wood bench seats they yanked their shoes off before slotting each leg into their leather fire-boots.

"What's that you got on?" Barry shouted above the screaming engine.

"That thing on your head?"

My fire-helmet was already perched on my head. It resembled that of an ancient Roman soldier.

"Is that the best you can do? Good job its dark," Barry laughed.

Confused by all the rush and now feeling embarrassed, I dressed as best I could.

Our appliance hit the rush hour traffic. With siren wailing and bell sounding we darted in and out disturbing other traffic but avoiding it as easily as if we were in a dodgem car. Barry went forward into the cab, removing his helmet to reveal his tight red curls. He clambered through the two open sliding doors that separated us on the outside from those in the front cab.

"We're backing up Weaver Road Fire Station to a house fire in their station area," Sub Officer told Barry.

Weaver Road Fire Station was one of Torridge City's outer Fire Stations; its district stretched to the outskirts of the city. Our driver continued through busy traffic with the ease and aplomb of a man with great experience and confidence. The dark cold winter air rushed by as we raced on. My two-fellow crew-members stood on the narrow rear platform. Gripping onto handrails, their situation looked precarious as we swung from side to side. The passing scenery flashed by so fast it was difficult to be sure in which direction we travelled. At last we arrived, our bell still clanging but the noise of the siren petering out. Another fire-appliance, presumably from Weaver Road Fire Station, stood outside a house. We pulled up alongside as firemen from the other appliance ambled down the garden path.

"Mickey," it had been a malicious fire-call they shouted.

All that rush and excitement for nothing!

On the journey back to the Station I felt drained. It had been so pointless and wasteful. Rest of the crew cursed anybody who made such calls.

"Here, wear this!" Barry said when we arrived back.

From one of the pegs in the muster-room he produced a modern helmet borrowed from one of the appliance drivers. Drivers, Barry told me, only wore flat caps and tunics when turning out and always left their fire-helmets behind. Now I looked like any other fireman.

The third day of my first tour on duty Wednesday did not bring another turnout. Fires, Barry tried to explain, did not come with any particular regularity.

"It's usually all or nothing," he said.

Our three weekdays on duty ended on Wednesday evening; our three nights began Thursday 1800 hours.

Barry advised me to bring some sheets to protect and cover the rough grey blankets, which were supplied when I first joined. A change of underwear was also recommended. I obediently brought these as he had suggested I should and stacked my spare clothing in the personal locker I was given. At every change of watch every appliance needed checking. Still working alongside Barry Bleck, I followed his every move like a lost lamb. We opened every locker door on the Pump Escape as our fifteen-hour night began.

After checking the appliances, we had an hour's drill. It was a cold dark night, so we assembled inside and prepared to listen to an officer reading from the Manuals of Firemanship books. These were our gospel. First published in 1943 by the Home Office, each of the nine manuals covered every subject describing every aspect of the service in minute detail. The warmest room on the Station was the long-room. The open coke fire had been allowed to burn down, but strenuous efforts were made to load the fire up again with several buckets of coke, which crackled and spit as the flames slowly took hold. Sub Officer Gardon, who had thinning grey hair and a face with eyes that bulged out from his sockets, was designated to do the reading. Droning on a single note he began.

I sat with the rest of White Watch as the Sub Officer droned on, reading every word from the Manual of

Firemanship Part, 6b. He regularly interrupted his reading by producing a small silver tin from inside of his uniform jacket. Taking a pinch of snuff between his thumb and first finger, he placed it first on the back of his wrist and inhaled the powder with gusto and relish. After these brief interludes he resumed, still reading in a boring manner. As he reached the bottom of the second page, the words 'eye-eye' went unnoticed. Page 'eye-eye-eye' caused a little amusement to those bothering to listen but when he reached page four, 'eye-v' caused uproar.

He ignored our laughter. Pausing to take more snuff, he carried on regardless. By the time he finished in his boring drone at seven o'clock, reaching 'eye x' (the Roman numerals) the reading session had proved entertaining if not educational.

Following the lecture, we were allowed to stand down. Again, I followed Barry closely, not knowing exactly what was expected.

"Stand down," he explained, "is the time left to us when all the routine work is completed."

Most of White Watch had disappeared. Some watched television, some played snooker and some sat around the coke fire. The warm and friendly atmosphere matched the heat from fire. By nine o'clock the fire glowed white hot making the room more like a games room than a place of work, and this was even more so when a sliding shutter door opened at nine o'clock to reveal a licensed bar.

"Don't drink on your first few nights," Barry advised.

Station Officer Finnan appeared for the first time since the parade only for the hour when the bar was open. He noticed the glass of lemonade in my hand and smiled in approval.

'Boots off' came at around midnight. My bed was in the main dormitory, itself a room converted from a wartime air raid shelter. I laid out my cotton sheets on the bed and covered them with the three grey blankets. The single metal-framed beds were positioned close together and covered with a horsehair mattress. The beds were so close together that you could easily reach out and touch your neighbour.

"You'll need your three blankets. It feels like another cold night," Barry told me.

I listened with one ear for the alarm bells, and it was a long time before I slipped into a shallow sleep.

I awoke sharply. Bells clanging and light from an electric bulb dragged me from my slumber. Men all around instinctively dropped their legs into their ready boxed-boots. Boxed-boots were made by feeding a pair of trousers over a pair of fire-boots leaving the tops open and ready for leaping into.

I was sleeping in my shirt and socks and underwear. I slotted both feet into my fire-boots, pulled up my trousers and with the braces over my shoulders I was dressed and ready. No one said a word while all this was going on.

I followed the others as we dashed from our dormitory outside down the street and finally into the muster-room. Most firemen slept well away from the engine house but Pump One crew always slept on portable beds in the muster-room and manned the appliance turning out regardless of any orders given during our parade at the beginning of the shift! It was considered faster and more efficient to have a crew sleeping immediately next to the engine house and our individual tallies so carefully positioned alongside the detailed appliances at 1800 hours was just ignored during sleeping hours. A practice, I was told, originating from the distant past when turnouts required harnessing the horses!

The Pump Two indicator light shone brightly from the board. The crew-members sleeping in the muster-room were already in the process of turning out. The appliance left the engine house, leaving behind it an empty bay thick with exhaust fumes.

We waited patiently in the muster-room for their return. At three o'clock in the morning I found myself struggling to stay awake. Yet still no one spoke.

Two of our officers, Sub Officer Gardon and Station Officer Finnan, eventually appeared from Brigade Control.

"Midden on fire, Mount Ribble Flats," Station Officer Finnan explained.

At last a rattle on the engine house doors signalled the return of Pump Two. Eager to learn about the turnout, I excitedly questioned a fireman but he only said.

"Time they got rid of those rubbish bins." It was an anti climax as everybody trailed off back to bed.

The dormitory now resumed its silence disturbed only by an occasional cough and the regular rhythm of someone snoring at the far end of the room. I was unable to drift off to sleep again listening to every noise. But I was startled as lights came on and bells started ringing. I was already awake and so I was into my fire-boots before anyone else moved. Amid groans of disbelief we all dashed out, ran outside and down the street taking us from the dormitory towards the main part of the Station, and once again lurched into the muster-room where we found that Pump One and Pump Escape were to go to a house fire.

For us, detailed as crew on Pump Two, it was our duty again to wait. During boots-off period we were the crew that did not turnout initially but were required to sit and wait in the muster-room in case of other turnouts.

We smelt the sweet cocktail of fire, which drifted when both crews eventually returned. The crews re-stocked their appliances, but still produced nothing by way of conversation.

"Teach them to smoke in bed," someone said, almost in passing.

Once more we all trailed off back to bed. When reveille arrived at six forty-five precisely I felt shattered. Disturbed nights, I discovered, were not easy. And with my first tour of duty ended there was still no exciting story to relate.

As our three days and three night's tours of duty multiplied, I felt more at ease. All the White Watch crew appeared friendly and I was able to put more names to faces as time progressed. It took time to meet everybody since someone was always on holiday, and with groups on leave spread across the whole calendar, it was rare to find the whole crew on duty at the same time.

As the new boy on White Watch I was fodder for practical jokes. Initiation ceremonies for new boys were common. As I had previously worked on building sites, such things were not entirely unknown to me. Now when going to the toilet I commonly expected objects to fly over the door. If the door was open then flying mops buckets or anything else to hand could be seen before they hit the unsuspecting stooge going about his business. One of the old hands on White Watch, with over seventeen year's service, Fireman Jeffrey Twaite, guided me through the maze of these potential hazards.

Jeffrey had served several years in the Royal Navy in submarines before joining the Fire Brigade all those years ago. Jeffrey's face was now tight and rarely broke into a smile.

"There is no such thing as toilet doors in submarines," he told me.

I was already reluctant to go to the toilet and such stories made me even more so. Should alarm bells sound, what was I to do? But long hours on duty meant there must be a time when nature called.

"If you really must go," Jeffrey warned, "then use the toilet nearest the engine house and keep the door open!" he added.

Jeffrey, a large framed man who was almost bald, had to believed. I took careful note of what he said. As nature called I selected the particular toilet he suggested and sat nervously with the door wide open. Nothing untoward happened. It was a little draughty but seemed safe from flying objects. However, I was to discover that I should not have believed him, for when the time came to pull the chain I first heard a muffled flushing noise and looked with horror at the basin as white creamy foam began to fill it to the brim. I watched with dismay as it began to overflow, but still the foam multiplied. It cascaded onto the floor, over the top of the basin and over the toilet-seat. A large creamy-white blanket spilled out of the cubicle and smothered everything in its path. Jeffrey, of course, just happened to be passing. A glint in his eyes and a large smile covered his face producing lines like creases in an old used shirt. Using two chemicals, aluminium sulphate and bicarbonate of soda, which were used in our foam extinguishers, he had placed one of the chemicals in the basin, and the other in the header tank. Brought together, they produced carbon dioxide gas and thick creamy foam.

As winter eased into spring tours of duty gathered momentum, turn-outs became a common place occurrence. At long last issued with a cap badge I slowly became an accepted member of White Watch.

As the daylight hours lengthened, the dread of attending Brigade Training School for the twelve weeks Recruits Course became a talking point for the members of the watch.

Training School, held at another of Torridge Stations, Ellen Approach Fire Station, was something to be feared. I heard rumours of the horrors of hook-ladders, of the exhausting and demanding breathing apparatus training and the dread of the carry down. All these terms were as yet unknown to me, and they were told with a good deal of intimidation and with a certain amount of glee and satisfaction.

Torridge City Fire Brigade adopted a policy of allowing recruits to serve three or four months on a Fire Station before being given this training. For these months we were watched carefully on the Station to see if we were made of the right material and were worthy of the cost of further training.

I suppose I must have passed this entry test since I was given May, just four months after joining, for my twelve weeks course.

As May came closer I became more and more familiar with station life. Arriving on duty early at 1730 hours, I changed into my uniform. At 1800 hours the usual parade and roll call designated me again as a crew-member on Pump Two. As I was opening every locker and accounting for every piece of listed equipment, the station bells sounded. Out of the small door from Brigade Control a woman appeared.

"Job Out, City centre. Off Washburn Street." Her voice was almost drowned by the sound of alarm bells.

"Another 999 coming in," she raised her voice.

The engines of Pump One, Pump Escape, and Turntable Ladder started, adding to the noise and excitement. Within seconds these three appliances shot out of the engine house. Their bays were left vacant. We closed all the engine house doors as residue from the exhaust of the appliances filled the engine house. Bells and sirens diminished in the distance as all three appliances disappeared down the street.

Prepared and dressed in our tunics and boots, and me still with the borrowed fireman's helmet in my hand, we gathered outside the Control Room door and waited. Sub Officer Gardon opened the Control Room door, forbidden territory for us, and went in. The tension grew as we peered through the crack of the open door.

At last one of the two women control officers grabbed a hand microphone. A garbled message spluttered through the radio system.

"From Station Officer Finnan at Washburn Street. Building well alight. Make Pumps five."

Make Pumps five meant additional appliances were needed at the fireground. With two Pumps already in attendance, the officer in charge requested a further three Pumps.

With siren wailing and with bells clanging our Pump Two, screaming in second gear, turned into Washburn Street, which was blocked by clouds of black, putrid smoke coming from a building at the far end of a block of shops.

This was to be my first experience of a large city centre fire.

Chapter 4

As we entered Washburn Street thick black smoke was belching out from a second-floor window and then curling majestically upwards. Sitting on the back of our Pump Two, we had arrived at the scene of a major fire in response to a 'Make Pumps Five', a further call for assistance. The thick smoke blocked our path.

A Leading Fireman, wearing his black helmet with its single red-band around the rim, emerged from the smoke and ran towards us.

"Water! We need more water," he cried.

A length of delivery hose from a stand-pipe poking out from the centre of the road snaked in a large bight before connecting into the Pump Escape. This was one of the two appliances that had arrived at the scene, answering the initial call. The delivery hose was of sufficient diameter to enable firemen to transfer water in quantity from one place to another.

Station Officer Finnan, his white helmet tilted at a crazy angle, approached our Pump as we shuddered to a halt.

"Kevin. We need more water," he screamed to Sub Officer Gardon, the officer in charge of Pump Two who was sitting in the front cab.

"It's a wholesale paint store! The buildings are full of fuel just waiting to go up!" he continued.

"There are more Pumps coming. Try the 'fire-tank' down Swale Road!" These were the Station Officer's final words before he spun round and half-walked, half-ran back towards the smoke, which now engulfed everything in its path.

Our Pump Two, complete with its crew of four, lurched forward and bounced over a length of hose on the road. Several Firemen from the two appliances already in attendance scurried around. It looked totally confusing.

We raced down Washburn Street, past the front of the burning shop. The heat from the fire hit our faces like heat from an opened-oven door. The oil-based paint was already feeding the fire.

We jerked to a halt in Swale Road, and Sub Officer Gardon sat alongside our driver, Fireman Robert Ray who was in the front cab, climbed down after flinging open his door.

"The fire-tank-lid is somewhere around here," he said.

Fire-tanks were underground holes in the road. Built for war-time-blitz conditions, these specially built brick lined caverns were positioned close to large size city-water mains. There were over fifty such tanks dotted all over Torridge City and their exact location often became a test question asked by the experienced firemen.

"That's it. Over there!" someone shouted, recognising a square steel lid in the middle of the road. Our Dennis F8 Pump Two stopped; it's rear-end sat over the lid.

"Tank lid keys, somebody?" came a query.

I knew what tank lid keys were, steel handles with a square end for fitting into a lid. There were stored in the nearside locker with rest of the water gear. Lifting the locker door and locking the safety catch which locked it in place; I reached inside for the two keys. Grabbing them I ran back to the fire-tank.

The driver of our appliance, Fireman Robert Ray and the Sub Officer struggled to get both keys into the two square holes in the lid. They were solid with grit; the handles would not fit.

"Float it off!" Robert suggested, his dark ginger hair falling over his eyes.

Suddenly a large dull explosion made us all look back to the fire. The paint shop front display window exploded. Large flying pieces of glass hung in the air refusing to fall. Hanging, almost floating they slowly crashed, then hit the road and bit into the lines of delivery hose. Dull muffled bangs echoed from within the fire, as further stocks of paint exploded. Flames fuelled by a sudden entrain of air escaped from the shattered window and water sprayed out from the damaged hose.

"Get this lid off!" Someone screamed.

With the inlet water valve for the tank turned on, air began to hiss out of the road surface around the edges of the lid. As air pressure built up inside the fire-tank, the hissing increased. Water seeped out. Then as the mains water filled the underground tank its lid gave way suddenly and ever so gently bobbed on the surface of the water. The lid was now loose and free, and a sideways push exposed the inside of the tank. Water oozed out from the chasm.

With guidance from our driver and crew I helped to fit two lengths of hard suction hose, stiff tubes with large brass screw fittings on each end, to the Pump inlet. A brass strainer screwed on to the end of the suction hose completed this part of the operation. Thick black tubing, looking like an elephant's trunk, now linked the water in the fire-tank to the Pump inlet.

The driver primed our pump, removing all the air from suction hose. Robert, the driver pushed the hand lever, situated next to the throttle lever, down firmly.

The engine laboured as the primer created a vacuum in the pump and the lengths of suction hose. With one end of the suction hose now underwater, all the air in the pump and suction hose was soon replaced by water from the fire-tank.

"Help me run out some hose." Robert panted. He peered at me through the strands of hair covering his eyes. Overwhelmed by all the commotion I followed him and did precisely what I was told.

We ran lengths of hundred-foot long and two and three-quarters inch in diameter delivery hose to the fire-ground. Joining several lengths of delivery hose together, we snapped the male and female brass couplings into each other until at last Pump Two, situated over two hundred yards away, and were finally connected to the Pump Escape positioned at the fireground. Robert ran back and opened the outlet valve on our Pump. The flat delivery hose swelled and expanded with the internal pressure. Water now filled our empty hose. Snaking and weaving, the delivery hose curled in large loops up the road. As I saw this happening a loud ringing bell disturbed me. I looked up.

A Turntable Ladder with a huge brass radiator at the front of a long bonnet with the word 'Leyland' in large letters charged towards us, up Swale Road. A large shiny brass bell hung from nearside of an open cab. The officer in charge, sitting on the left of the driver, shook the leather handle of the brass bell vigorously to clear a path for the arrival of a second Turntable Ladder.

"Get all this hose pulled to one side." I heard a shout and looked up to see a very senior officer indeed, the Assistant Chief Officer, Mr Carp. He was tall and thin and dressed in a flat uniform cap. His tunic, which had full chrome epaulettes on both shoulders, was unbuttoned.

"You, YOU, young 'laddie'," he shouted at me.

"You can be the monkey, laddie!"

I assumed he wanted me to climb on the ladder.

The Turntable Ladder stopped on the opposite side of the road. The driver dismounted from his open cab quickly and proceeded to lower the supporting jacks. I watched as he swung each of the four hinged jacks out, away from the body. They clanked against their stops. He placed a thick piece of wood underneath each steel foot and turned the handles to let the four supporting feet down to the road surface. Finally, he tightened each of the four jacks, and expertly turned all the screw handles until the heavy Turntable Ladder rested evenly on the road surface.

"Get yourself a belt" he said to me gruffly. The driver looked old, and the ordeal of bringing this monster of a fire-engine from Weaver Road Fire Station, which was a good six miles away, had obviously taken a great deal of physical effort.

This particular type of turntable table ladder, a 'Leyland Merryweather', was one in the UK distributed by the Home Office at the beginning of World War 2. Previously these Leyland appliances had Metz (German) ladders fitted but on the onset of War, English manufactured Merryweather ladders were commissioned.

Under the seat I found a thick belt with black and red stripes and with a large hook attached to it. The belt supported two sets of straps and buckles and took a few seconds to be tightened and fitted around my waist.

The self-supporting ladder was elevated, lifting away from the housed gantry and extended, shooting upwards. Its head continued to be extended until it stopped high above the road, and positioned away from the burning building. I glanced at the blazing shop. Radiated heat hit us from the fire just twenty yards away. Black heavy smoke enclosing ribbons of red flame curled upwards from the broken windows.

I was now belted and dressed and ready to climb up the ladder. The delivery hose supplied from a nearby Pump snaked around the base of the Turntable Ladder and went straight up to the top. It swelled as it filled with water.

"Wait until the water arrives at the top of the ladder," the driver told me, "then walk up slowly. If it gets too hot, stop and come down. But if you get to the top, fasten yourself with the hook."

I accepted every word without question. I knew it was dangerous to propel a man up to a fire on an extending ladder. Hidden pockets of heat and unseen objects made it far safer to climb the ladder after it was in position.

I experienced difficulty at first as I climbed from the four-foot high operator's platform to the base of the ladder. I swung myself out before I could catch hold of the sides of the ladder. Once I was on the ladder, the rungs were not easy to find. The delivery hose running up the ladder snaked and zigzagged over its whole width, making it difficult to climb. From the base of the ladder each of its four extensions narrowed. I struggled upwards until I reached the head of the ladder.

On the last and the final extension, the ladder narrowed to shoulder width. I located a small ring, but I needed to lean in close to allow the hook on my belt to fit on to it. Leaning out and waving at the driver operator below, I indicated I was now hooked in position. A voice squeaked into life from a round metal canister below my left shoulder.

"Drop the platform and show your heels," the driver told me.

I looked at my feet. A steel platform was bolted to the side of the ladder next to my left boot. I undid the bolt and as I moved my feet in turn the platform at last fell into position. Now standing on the platform, both my heels stuck out and were visible to the driver below.

This indicated to the operator below that my toes were safe. Should the ladder need to be extended or lowered; my toes remained free and would not be trapped in any moving parts. The driver began to train, or turn, the ladder. It jerked to the right and turned closer to the building.

A jet of water shot out of the brass nozzle at the top of the ladder and crackled as the air trapped inside was forced out and forwards under pressure. Water leaked from the joint on the nozzle and trickled back down a large wooden handle.

The large handle provided ample vertical movement but allowed only a small movement to the sides.

Fastened securely, seventy foot up in the air, the ladder slowly moved closer over the fire. Water shot out from the head of the ladder as I experimented by moving the large wooden control handle up and down.

I could see firemen scurrying about on the ground below. Huge crowds of spectators had gathered in the street. The police were trying to marshal the crowds away from the danger. Fire appliances, looking like small red toys, stood together. The roads were glossy with water.

A slight rumble drew my eyes back to the fire. Smoke percolated through every seam in the slate roof tiles which were still intact. The noise reached a crescendo, but still it increased. The roof began to move. Slowly, almost too slowly, slates began to peel away, sliding down before reaching the guttering and flying off to the ground below. A single flame pierced the gaps left by the disappearing slates. Suddenly, without warning, half the roof caved inwards. More slates slid off over the edge and hurtled to the ground. I could only watch as the Firemen below, alerted by the rumbling from inside the building, and ran from the now impending danger.

I felt the stab of hot air strike my face. A squeaky voice crackled through the communication system.

"All right," it asked. I muttered that it was getting hot.

The ladder now trained to the left and slowly edged away from the roof. Flames shot out from the open roof and almost immediately a gush of hot air struck the side of my face. Water, now leaking from the nozzle, was very welcome; it kept my face cool.

The ladder was trained back once more over the fire. I looked down.

Assistant Chief Fire Officer Carp, now dressed in a black helmet with a chrome rim and a big black oil-skin knee length jacket and green waders, made his way slowly up the ladder which flexed and dipped slightly back and forth as his additional weight altered its balanced position.

"What's your name, laddie?" he asked when he reached the top. I told him.

"Now Fairn," he said shouting to be heard above the noise of the water jet shooting out in front of us and climbing higher. He forced me forwards against rungs of the ladder.

"Keep that jet of water on that adjoining wall. The shop and building have gone." His words spilled out.

"We have to stop it spreading next door." He stood close behind me, pressing me tight against the ladder and breathing on my neck under the rear brim of my helmet.

"Forget about the flames. Just keep that jet of water hitting that wall."

I tried to turn around to see his face, but we were too close to each other. His hands gripped both sides of the ladder, pinning me down. Thinking I was doing so well by attacking the flames, I had never thought of preventing the fire spreading.

After studying the area, the Assistant Chief began his climb back to the ground. He parted from me with words of encouragement.

"You're doing all right," he said, his words tailing off as he descended.

The roof had now gone completely and each floor followed in rapid succession. Debris showered all around. Bricks, slates, wooden beams all crashed landing onto the street below. My jet of water continued to pour from seventy foot up on to the adjoining wall.

The leak from the nozzle continued. A trickle of water ran down the inside of my tunic sleeve, down my trouser leg, and finally into my left boot. Shuffling to one side only filled my right boot. As daylight turned slowly to dusk I was still directing the water jet onto the adjoining wall. Some water even went down some of the chimney pots on the next building; scarred by fire, they looked like massive salt and pepper cruets. Gallons of water from my jet continued to drench the party wall. Eventually the jet lost its pressure as the water was finally turned off.

"You can come down now," the speaker crackled and the words were welcome.

"You've been up that ladder nearly three hours!" The driver greeted me as I reached terra firma at last. I was wet, cold and stiff.

"Good job. Well done lad!" He told me.

Chief Officer Bass, in charge of the whole incident, sent a stop message, indicating that no further appliances or assistance were required, by radio to the Brigade Control.

This large City centre fire was considered serious enough to warrant our Chief, Assistant Chief, eight Pumps, and two Turntable Ladders being involved. Ten Pumps were the maximum Torridge City could muster. Any more appliances had to be called from outside Torridge City, but this was never encouraged. It cost money for another Fire Brigade to give assistance, and anyway calling for such outside help was an admittance of defeatism.

The shell of the building, where the fire had been, steamed and died. It was gaunt and dead, but the surrounding property had been saved from the fire, which was prevented from spreading. Now the long damping-down procedure commenced.

Sub Officer Gardon found me and explained that Pump Two and its crew were to return to the Station for a quick change of clothing.

Since the Pump Two we turned out with originally was still connected to the fire-tank we found another appliance, and returned to our Fire Station. We washed, changed our underwear, and donned fresh trousers and dry fire-tunics as well as a fresh pair of fire-boots. After a gulp of hot sweet tea, we were back at the fire within the hour, our glory now long gone.

The huge crowd, which had gathered to witness our battle, had now dispersed, and the unenviable task of damping down for the next few hours began.

The building was completely gutted. The front wall had collapsed completely. The rear and one of the sides were severely damaged, but the shop on one side looked intact. Protection from my jet from the Turntable Ladder had perhaps helped in some way and stopped the spreading fire. From my position high above the fire-ground I had witnessed tremendous team-work as the crews below gained control over such a major incident. As more supplies of water were obtained, the sheer workload and the strenuous effort carried out by all was a credit to everyone involved.

Heat from the body of the shop, which had been destroyed, was considerable. Most of the roof and upper floors had collapsed into the cellar, where steam from the jets of water aimed into the cellar indicated there were pockets of fire hidden beneath the tons of rubble.

Midnight passed and still, four Pumps with twenty men remained, carrying out damping-down duties. We continued to pour gallons of water into the steaming cellar before being relieved at 0430 hours. We returned to Torridge City Station, tired and wet. Our Pump Two, which had been rescued at last from its position at the fire-tank, needed re-equipping with clean delivery hose. Every length of delivery hose which had been used at a fire needed washing before it was hung up to dry in the heated hose tower. This would be done later since our Station carried sufficient lengths of spare hose to re-equip each of the Pumps twice over. The appliance also needed to be filled with petrol and to be washed down before anyone could relax.

In the early morning hours, it took some coaxing for us to move our aching bones and weary bodies. It had been a long, long night. I had a glimpse into the amount of hard work and courage that Firemen had to have. When they were called on, they performed without hesitation.

Arriving home that morning after the end of my long night on duty at 0900 hours, being able to slide between clean sheets into a comfortable bed was shear pleasure. For a few seconds the excitement of the night was re-enacted before the pull of unconsciousness dragged me into a deep and welcome sleep.

On the next night and back on duty, all members of our watch retold own stories and relived the night of our large fire. Morale on the Station increased noticeably. A busy Station is a happy one, I learned.

With my bulging kit bag filled with two pairs of boots, tunics, a borrowed chrome axe, overalls, uniform cap, undress jacket and trousers, it was time for me to attend Brigade Training School at Ellen Approach Station. Sadly, I parted company with White Watch; I had been working with them for four months. I hoped to be back if I could pass the rigours and pitfalls of the Training School requirements.

Chapter 5

Snivelling-Monday arrived.

It was my first day at Training School. Torridge City Fire Brigade Training School was situated at Ellen Approach Fire Station, and provided facilities for the training of recruits for Torridge and also for the surrounding County Borough Fire Brigades.

Thirty-six of us cowered beneath a glass canopy, sheltering from the incessant drizzle.

We met the Assistant Divisional Officer, the Commandant of the Training School and three Sub Officers; all four were to grill and drill us for the next twelve weeks.

One rank above a Station Officer, Assistant Divisional Officer Grayling his uniform cap pressed firmly on his head, marched amongst us. His three large impellers on each shoulder looked like six steel nipples pointing up. An impeller was a distinction used in all officers' rank markings.

It was the size of a large button and one of its features was taken from the internal workings of the Fire Service water pumps.

He looked kind, almost benign. He stood tall, smart and erect in his immaculate uniform. We shuffled nervously, straining to get our first glimpse of the full entourage of training officers.

Sub Officer Roach, the second in command, carried the reputation of being a tyrant. This reputation was fuelled by rumours that he was a no-nonsense man and a strict disciplinarian. His military service record was exemplary, and the mere thoughts of being taught by the loudest drill Sergeant ever, sowed seeds of fear and dread in us. On his left stood Sub Officer Hussar who was rumoured to be an eccentric professor, with idiosyncrasies that burdened on the insane. On his square face, under his thin pointed nose, he sported a pencil-lined moustache. His head repeatedly jerked rapidly to the right.

Two paces behind these three stood Sub Officer Brill, younger and new to the Training School. Until recently he had been a Leading Fireman on Torridge City Station's Blue Watch. He had taken this new position in order to reach the second rung on the promotion ladder. With a grin that grew and creased his cheeks he seemed young, and almost out of place compared with the rest of the ancient instructors standing in front of him. Suddenly the snivelling Monday sky blubbered. Raindrops the size of glass beads rattled and bounced off the floor of the drill yard. I stood nervously with the rest of the squaddies, taking shelter from the deluge. I extracted my bulging kit bag from the enormous pile, which looked like elephant seals mating under the glass canopy.

Twelve of the thirty-six recruits like me were from the City of Torridge. The other twenty-four were from other City Fire Brigades. Their respective Brigades paid the fees for their own recruits. These fees helped to finance the running costs of the school. Of the five recruits who had enrolled with me in January only two now remained. Many men joined the Fire Brigade, but other employment was easy to obtain, often with better pay and no night work, so most of them did not last through the three months induction period.

"What's this? You look like a flock of shaggy sheep!" Sub Officer Roach's voice boomed at us. One point of the rumours proved correct.

"Get fell in outside on the drill ground."

Like sheep we shuffled into the deluge.

"YOU, YOU" he screamed at someone close to me.

"Yes, YOU!" he yelled even louder.

"Stand here. The rest of you fall in alongside!

"This is a uniformed and disciplined service." His voice rose louder and louder. We moved obediently into position.

"From the right, dress!"

We shuffled into position. I looked and at those who knew and copied them. My arm was outstretched and my knuckles touched those of the next fireman to the right.

"Open order, march!"

The men alongside me stepped forward one pace. Belatedly I copied them.

"Right. Your names?"

Roach marched along the line. His shoes gleamed; his uniform was smart, immaculate. The rank markings of a Sub Officer sparkled with the raindrops that dropped from his uniform cap onto his shoulders. As each of us answered to our name he looked at his list and detailed our squad colour and our instructor.

"Fairn," Sub Officer Roach shouted in my left ear, "you're in Red Squad."

Sub Officer Brill, one pace behind Roach, grasped a brown cardboard box whose lid deepened in colour as rain soaked into the lid.

Tilting the lid to protect the contents, he presented each of us with a small metal tally, which removed carefully from the box. This was our personal identification number

47

for the duration of the course and was to be worn at all times. As I unclipped the safety pin and struggled in the wet to locate the clasp I noticed the number ten in flaking blue and painted roughly on the well-used disc.

Assistant Divisional Officer Grayling was at attention patiently waiting in front of the line of bedraggled men. Rain still drummed down from a heavy sky.

"My name is Assistant Divisional Officer Grayling," he began.

His uniform cap positioned with precision and perfectly level, supported a small puddle on its top. Growing with every drop of rain, the puddle threatened to overflow.

"The reputation of your Brigade is at stake," his voice went on, soft and delicate. Straining to hear, I expected at any moment that the water would cascade all over him.

"During the next twelve weeks you will pass or fail. If you pass you'll be a basic fireman. If you fail you'll be a civilian again looking for another job."

He turned smartly to the left and marched away. In total defiance of all normal rules of gravity the pool of water never moved off the top of his cap as he disappeared from our sight.

"Fall out!" Sub Officer Roach shouted.

We turned to our right and shuffled like wet rats from the soaked drill ground; we were now to collect our kit bags. With steam rising from our sodden bodies we entered the corridor and went to our lockers. We passed a large glass fronted notice board on the way.

"Study this notice board at all times," Sub Officer Roach suddenly stopped us and ordered.

Those at the front, keen and eager suddenly halted. Those of us following behind then crashed into each other. Our heavy bulky kit bags fell with a damp thud to the floor.

"By reading it you will find exactly what you should be doing and what you must wear." He marched on.

Looking through the glass panel we strained to see our instructions and to learn the details of every lesson in the first week.

For all drill sessions we were to be in flat caps, tunics and boots. Walking-out uniform, the so-called undress uniform, was to be worn at meal times and for classroom lectures, and during the morning and afternoon break times. Routines and cleaning periods were to be carried out in overalls and flat caps. With precise organisation, no two sessions followed which required the same dress. Every change meant a dash to our lockers to re-dress in the appropriate gear and a mad dash back again.

Every morning would begin on the drill ground with an hour's squad-drill; we had to be dressed in overalls, shoes and flat caps. There was something special every Wednesday morning, requiring us to be dressed in our best tunics, flat caps, polished leather boots, belt and axe. On that day every week, Assistant Divisional Officer Grayling would inspect us.

Picking our kit bags up again, we all left the all-important notice and went to the locker room. We changed quickly from our soaking clothes into dry overalls. By the end of our first day any dry clothes were now thoroughly soaked as a result of constantly changing in and out of wet uniforms.

"Quick. Quick," a voice, now easily recognisable, barked at us again and again.

Recruits from all the visiting Brigades slept at the school in dormitories converted from rooms, which served as lecture rooms during the day. As favoured Torridge City men, we were allowed home for the night. For this privilege we were given extra cleaning routines to be carried out before we left. We also provided waiter service, dishing out the meagre food allowance to the school of hungry recruits.

The first day over, I arrived home damp but still keen. I thought Mother would be keen to hear my story. But she had retreated into one of her silent moods. Her full history remains an enigma, even now. She never discussed the reason we came to England when she was struggling, heavily pregnant with me. Although she still retained an accent, she otherwise spoke and understood English perfectly. Occasionally, especially when she was upset, she chattered away to herself in German, but she always insisted that I spoke English. Regardless of many taunts and racial abuse, she worked hard taking in washing, cleaning, and doing anything to make enough money for basic living. She never complained.

The Fire Brigade wages meant a drop in my weekly wage packet from my previous job, but I gave her all I had. Mother and I were very close. I understood how she felt, sat and ate my dinner on my own.

Day two. The rain still poured down from a dark miserable sky. Morning parade was followed by an hour of marching. Dressed in the appropriate rig as detailed on the notice board overalls, flat uniform cap, we were subjected to more shouting from Sub Officer Roach and to another soaking from the relentlessly crying sky.

Louder and louder the commands kept coming.

"You are a complete shambles! Stand in line!" Roach's face grew crimson with rage.

Marching and squad drill was new to me. Pressure was on those who served their national service to bring rest of us, born too late for compulsory conscription, into line. The Fire Service followed the Navy for the style of saluting, standing to attention and marching. Our undress uniform with double-breasted buttons down the front was also similar in colour and design to that worn by some Navy personnel.

We were told that 'Squad Shun!' meant that we must stand with our heels together and feet turned out at an angle of forty-five degrees. Our knees were to be straight, our bodies erect, and heads up. Shoulders were to be level and square to the front. The palms of both hands had to be turned and positioned towards the thighs with the hands partially closed the thumb close to the forefinger. We were to look straight ahead.

When we were to stand at ease, we were to move the left leg twelve inches to the left, put our hands behind the back with the back of one hand in the palm of the other and grasped lightly with the fingers and thumb. This allowed both arms to hang easily at their full extent.

We tiptoed through the Fire Service Drill Book, learning to stand easy, number off, size a squad and to take each pace the correct length. We marched in quick time, in slow time; we stood and marked time. We marched in a squad. We had to do all this with precision and detail.

Those of us who were inexperienced and found difficulty with the marching held a broom handle which reached to the man in front. These were issued to co-ordinate the left leg and right arm, and resembled connecting rods from steam engines. A distant noise of railway engines puffing away came from within the ranks. This was not appreciated.

"If I find the man responsible for these childish noises, he will be playing trains permanently," Sub Officer Roach screamed at us.

Our first Wednesday arrived. The rain ceased at last. In full dress uniform of fire-tunics, fire-boots, belt, firemen's axe and flat uniform caps, we were ready for our full inspection. This was to be taken by Assistant Divisional Officer Grayling.

Every detail of our appearance was minutely inspected. In anticipation our hats were brushed and their peaks gleamed, our tunics were pressed, our buttons were clean and shiny and even the Torridge City coat of arms insignias on the buttons needed to be correctly aligned. Our belts were polished, the buckles expected to shimmer. Axes were held at arms' length, the handle bleached white and the axe head polished to shine like glass. Our trousers had to have knife-edge sharp creases and our boots had to be polished to resemble mirrors.

On that first Wednesday, most of our standards were well below requirements. I glanced down the line of recruits as the Assistant Divisional Officer and Sub Officer Roach, his notepad and pencil at the ready, stopped at each man in turn. Every item found not up to standard was noted and our numbers were taken.

Eventually they stood in front of me.

"Is that a borrowed axe?" Grayling asked.

My bright chromed fireman's axe, held proudly out in front, was indeed borrowed. Prior to training school one of old hands back on the Fire Station had lent me his specially treated axe to save me time in endless hours trying to bring the normal dull metal surface of the axe blade to that of a mirror.

"Where is your identification tally?"

There was no identification tally fastened to my tunic.

"Take Fairn's number, Sub Officer."

"What is your number?" Roach screamed. He wrote down 'ten' for further punishment.

Assistant Divisional Officer Grayling was not pleased at what he had seen. Things would have to improve. Those who had their numbers taken would suffer extra cleaning duties.

Classroom and a lecture always followed the morning squad drill and required yet another change of clothing. The lecture room was cramped for the thirty-six of us and thus created another mad rush to change from one set of clothes to another and to get a decent seat. From my schooldays I knew that there was always less chance of questions being directed to those at the front, than those sat at the back. I carefully made for an unpopular front seat.

"All change," 'Professor' Hussar announced as he entered the class room to give us his first lecture, following an hour's squad drill and change of clothes from overalls to undress uniform.

"Sit as per your recruit numbers starting at the back of the room," he jerked his head sideways. So, I found myself seated at the back of the classroom after all the pushing and moving of chairs. He began his first lesson on hydraulics.

For as long as I could remember I had struggled with sums and arithmetic. Now all the dreaded rules and formulas from my schooldays were resurrected. He mumbled on, his voice always at the same level, and boring. He brought a pile of old notes to every lecture and read every sheet of paper from top to bottom. He then turned each tatty sheet and kept them, no doubt for the next recruits' course. When and only when, the final sheet of paper had been read carefully from top to bottom did he finish his lecture.

To add colour to these dreary proceedings, the recruit who sat on my left suggested we counted the number of twitches he made in any given lecture. At each jerk he jolted his face to the right. His right cheek was screwed up and folds of skin were creased to form a hideous mass of wrinkles from his hairline to his cheekbone.

"Forty-three!" I counted.

After the lecture we changed once more into the correct attire and went back onto the drill ground. This brought relief as classroom theory gave place to practical exercises. Tuesdays and Thursdays were the nights for the Torridge City men to perform menial tasks, our tasks for the concession to being allowed to go home every night. We had to clean every floor, working on our hands and knees; even the Fireman's friend, the mop and bucket was considered too easy. We also had to polish every brass fitting in sight and make them gleam.

One of the floors we had to polish was in the canteen area, which was also part of the operational station. The operational canteen man on duty, Fireman Chevin, knew our routine and offered us assistance secretly. Kenneth 'Gripper' Chevin was a legend in the Brigade and well known through the efficient grapevine that transmitted all snippets of gossip. He was known to be strong, as befitted an ex-boxer.

Strangely he spoke in a high, squeaky voice, but we trusted him in spite of this.

"Someone needs to keep a look out," he sang to us with a glint in his eye as he produced a mop and bucket to make our task easier. In no time the floor was mopped and cleaned to perfection.

Sub Officer Roach was certainly not impressed when he returned suddenly, unannounced. He emptied the contents of our mop bucket onto the floor and stood hovering as we cleaned the floor again, this time by hand.

As that first week continued, we began basic hose running. All drills in the Fire Brigade Drill Manual were explained in detail. Each individual crew-member was given a number; numbers did everything. Numbers, we were told was essential to enable each man to perform a specific task.

Working through the official drill book, basic delivery hose drills began. The delivery hose was made from a heavy canvas outer skin and lined with thick rubber. Although it was only twenty-feet in length it weighed over forty pounds. The male coupling at one end and the female coupling at the other were made of solid brass. Cleaned to look like gold, we were told that these couplings were not to be thought of as brass, but of glass!

Changing numbers at every drill, we each learned to ship a standpipe. We removed the steel hydrant lid, screwed the large clumsy brass standpipe on the screw thread onto the water main, ran out three lengths of hose, fitted a large size nozzle into the female outlet and shouted the order 'water on'.

When we were given the order to Knock Off and Make Up, we rolled the hose back into a neat Swiss roll, unshipped the standpipe, replaced the hydrant lid and stored all the equipment neatly on the drill ground. Rubber lined hose was never designed to be neat and it always looked untidy.

As the crew's number one, I reported to Sub Officer Brill.

"Drill completed, Sir," indicated we had completed our allotted task.

"Carry on number one," Brill ordered.

I ran smartly back to join the other crew-members.

"Hose not rolled up properly. Roll it up again!" His smile, was it deceptive?

After another try the end result looked no better, but the second attempt seemed to satisfy him.

As the first week ended, Assistant Divisional Officer Grayling's parting speech did not give a very good picture of our performance. Things would have to improve, he announced.

The weekend, free of Training School restrictions, gave a welcome breathing space to the numbers game and to the strict regime, with someone watching and criticising every movement.

With an effort I attended the second week. My dread of another eleven weeks of such painfully slow instruction and unquestioning blind obedience brought grave doubts whether I should continue. I was bored. Already having served on a busy operational Fire Station and riding to fires and incidents, I had experienced the job at first hand. I had lived and ate with firemen who, for the first time in my life, treated me as an equal. Because of this I did find sufficient reasons to continue.

All the equipment we trained with was old and obsolete. Scaling ladders, sixty-foot wheeled escape ladders, trailer pumps, all were unknown in modern Fire Stations. Wartime appliances, more suitable for a museum than for modern day instruction, often struggled to get themselves out of the drill shed. One old Leyland Pump Escape, with an open cab and a heavy sixty-foot wheeled escape ladder, perched on its back, needed hand starting every morning. Plenty of volunteers raced forward to wind the starting handle and show their strength, only to find the compression from its six, cylinder; longstroke engine was too much to turn. Usually this farce concluded by all hands push-starting the monster into life.

In the classroom, under the auspices of our Sub Officers, we recorded pages and pages of information on the size, construction, and manufacture of ladders, hose and pumps, all in minute detail.

"The outer rims of the large wooden carriage or coach wheels, that carried the fifty and sixty-foot escapes, were made from wych-elm, the hubs in oak, and the spokes and felloes made from ash." I diligently recorded every precious word.

Once again in the prescribed dress on the drill ground, the numbers game continued. Detailed crew-numbers, which were changed until everyone eventually, had done each task in the drill.

Yet another ancient appliance, a 1940 Leyland Cub Pump, appeared on the drill ground. Twelve of us were divided into three groups of four.

I shouted my appropriate crew-number, three.

"Number One crew fall in!"

We ran smartly, positioning ourselves three paces away, facing the rear of the appliance as we were ordered.

"Mount!" was the order.

As instructed we climbed aboard the appliance smartly.

Number One in the left-hand front seat. Number two in the driver's seat. Number three and four sat in the rear. Then came the order.

"Change round!"

Number one jumped out from the nearside front, crashing his door behind him and climbed in the rear to become number three. Number two jumped out from his driving position, ran around the front of the appliance, opened the door, climbed aboard and slammed the door shut, becoming number one.

Number three shuffled across the cab seat and became number four. Number four jumped out from his position, opened the driver's door and became number two, closing yet another door with a bang.

This ritual of changing round from different positions and slamming doors must have been some use to somebody somewhere, but from our viewpoint as we charged from seat to seat it was hard to see any practical benefit derived from it!

But not all drills were of such poor quality. Wet drills when we used water were more realistic, and climbing ever-higher ladders gave us more confidence, which increased as the ladders got higher.

Our third week began, and we started the dreaded introduction to the hook-ladder.

A wooden hook-ladder was carried easily by one man from the drill shed and placed carefully on the ground in front of us. It looked simple in design. It was thirteen feet nine inches in length and weighed thirty pounds. From head of the ladder a large hook hinged out and locked in position. Sub Officer Brill picked up the ladder placed the protruding hook on to the first-floor window-sill of the drill tower. The ladder hung only by its hook. Leaning away from the wall he proceeded to climb the ladder. His outstretched arms relayed his weight through his feet to the toe-pieces, two small protruding metal brackets on the bottom of the ladder. It looked anything but safe.

Sub Officer Brill climbed with confidence and entered the first-floor window. Feeding the hook-ladder upward through his hands to the next window-sill, the ladder was suspended, once more, from its single hook. Climbing out of the window he scaled the ladder and entered the room on the second floor; his technique was impressive and he returned to the ground just as easily as he had gone up.

My first attempt was disastrous. The ladder swung off to one side.

"Your arms ought to act as if they are made of string!" The Sub Officer said, his grin just managing to part his lips.

The hook-ladder fulfilled its reputation. As our squad took it in turns to copy the excellent example of the Sub Officer we found the hook-ladder was a difficult piece of equipment to master. Most of the other drills involved working as a member of a crew, and if things went wrong the whole crew was suspect. But the hook-ladder relied on the individual to perform correctly. It was regarded on Fire Stations as not a practical piece of equipment but only as a training tool; anyone who could climb hook-ladders could climb anything.

For a brief period, I was no longer bored and looked forward to the sheer challenge of hook-ladders. But this surge of interest did not last long. Both in the classroom and on the drill ground things progressed far too slowly. With so much effort placed upon detail, with our constant changing into different dress and with the evening cleaning routines which had to meet such high standards, any useful knowledge became lost among the mass of trivia.

Occasionally, however we were given examples of real dangers.

For one of these, Sub Officer Brill organised a session away from the prison compound of the drill yard and took us to a small stream. Two lengths of delivery hose from the delivery outlets of the pump ran out along the grass bank and were left unmanned. Water from the stream was boosted through a trailer-pump, which allowed the pressure to increase until the nozzle outlet thrashed about. Like a venomous snake's head, it banged and thrust itself against the ground. Its full weight and power demonstrated the danger of being hit as the nozzle thudded in anger on the grass. Sub Officer Brill proceeded to tame the nozzle by following the line of the delivery hose from the pump. He crawled towards the raging outlet, and as he slowly crept towards it the thrashing decreased. Reaching the outlet, he obtained full control, and although he got thoroughly wet in the process he tamed the angry python.

This was a splash of colour during a dreary six weeks.

We were half the way through the course, and the ordeal of revising for the midway examinations loomed.

Chapter 6

Slowly, painfully slowly, the weeks dragged by. We faced the prospect of the halfway examinations and of another late Thursday when we stayed back to do the cleaning. The work was not hard but it was boring, tedious and only completed when the clock reached 1830 hours. All training school brasses, standpipes, hose-couplings, stored in the Training school drill hall needed to be regularly polished, until the finish looked like gold.

To demonstrate the application of 'Brasso', the metal polish, which was a fireman's constant accessory, our tyrant Sub Officer Roach, took time to rub and polish a single hose coupling.

"The trick of using Brasso is the actual putting on the liquid and rubbing it in," he told us, his hand working a Brasso dampened-rag on the coupling until a black wet gunge completely covered the surface. Left to dry, it became a white-grey powder, which rubbed off to reveal a glistening coupling. This was an example for us to copy.

"I'll be back in an hour," he promised. He walked away leaving shelves stacked high with brass implements with which to follow his example and reach his standard.

All the old appliances used for our instruction and drill were stored in the Training School drill hall. Among these ancient training school fire appliances stood several Home Office Green Goddess appliances, gathering dust. Kept in case of a future nuclear war and manned by volunteer auxiliary firemen, and firewomen, several of these green painted appliances were stored bumper to bumper along a rear wall. There was so little room that all the Training School Appliances competed for any available space.

Both our old Pump Escapes appliances carried wheeled escape ladders, their large carriage wheels hanging high and free and turned round easily. We were bored as we waited for the belated return of Sub Officer Roach.

"Spin the wheel," someone suggested. It was a daring challenge to occupy our time. The technique was to hold onto these large wheels by both arms, with legs wide apart. The hands gripped the spokes of the wheels; the legs were pressed firmly against the inside rim. The wheel was sent spinning; the greatest number of revolutions decided the winner. The challenge began, but one of the Green Goddesses was parked too close to another for its large carriage wheels to spin freely.

"Move it," someone suggested.

As quick as lightning I leaped into the cab, released the hand brake and with a big heave by willing hands, the green appliance lurched forward. I slammed on the foot brake only to find the pedal going flat to the cab floor. The appliance had not been used for some time and there was no air in the braking system. Before I could pull on the hand brake the machine kissed the wall.

Sub Officer Roach, as if by magic appeared at that moment. Examining the front mudguard for damage, he glowered at me.

"Another mark against you, number ten. Report to Assistant Divisional Officer Grayling, Fairn," he warned, able to put a name to my number as I emerged from the cab of the Green Goddess.

With the training course at the halfway stage, the Breathing Apparatus lectures began. Giving us the history of men wearing protection against smoke at fires, Sub Officer Hussar demonstrated an early example. From an old wicker basket, he produced a pair of leather bellows, a big red mask and a length of canvas covered rubber tubing. Men outside and well away from the fire worked the bellows, forcing fresh air through the tubes to the recipient wearing the hood inside a fire and relying on this help. He passed the heavy leather red painted copper riveted mask around for us all to examine. I pulled the hood over my face. The inside stank of stale prehistoric air.

There had been some improvements since those days and the oxygen Proto Mark Five, with a supply lasting for an hour, was to be our main training example of modern breathing apparatus. Carried operationally on many of our appliances in Torridge City Fire Brigade, Proto sets were considered by many of the older firemen to be far superior to the new, recently acquired, compressed air-sets.

The Proto Mark Five weighed twenty-seven pounds and pressed heavily on the shoulders on two leather straps.

A large rubber bag lay on the chest and the black-oxygen cylinder dug into the base of one's back. The set was completely enclosed, and supplies of oxygen entered the system from a cylinder containing compressed oxygen. A reducing valve allowed oxygen under high pressure to flow gently into the set. The wearer's exhaled breath entered into a rubber bag containing soda lime, which absorbed the carbon dioxide.

A sealed canister containing calcium chloride helped to reduce the temperature of the hot exhaled breath before the wearer breathed in again through a mouthpiece.

The set was regularly taken to pieces ritually, and every last washers, spring, nut and bolt was removed, examined and re-assembled. Great emphasis was placed upon the workings of the reducing valve and the exact and precise diameter of the hole, which held back the spring and controlled the oxygen's entry into the chamber under high pressure. This we were informed was very, very important. Thirteen and a half thousands of an inch, we dutifully recorded this vital information!

As the mid-way examinations loomed our brains became filled to capacity with knowledge. I struggled to transfer the painfully memorised knowledge into written answers as we sat for a whole day in the classroom. Questions from the blackboard bombarded me. No one failed, however as the results, posted on the notice board, showed. In fact, some bright spark achieved ninety-nine percent. My name bounced off the bottom in theory but was towards the top in practical drills.

This was a cause for celebration and a night out. Never slow to indulge in drunken revelry, and since it was not one of our nights for extra routines, I dashed home, gulped down the meal Mother had prepared in record time, returned and waited for the rest of the course members at the local public house. Two drinks in front.

As our pints went down the atmosphere became more congenial and the desire to have had better examination results became obscured beneath an alcoholic screen.

"What's a one-man band look like?" Someone asked.

I thought everyone must have seen a one-man band.

"I've never seen one. What do they look like?" Someone insisted.

I began to describe thus showing off my expert knowledge about how the different instrument was positioned.

To demonstrate the cymbals between the knees, I knocked my legs together. To show a mouth organ between the lips, I imitated blowing imaginary notes, complete with noises to match. With a big mythical drum on my back I swung my arms and made a drum noise as I pretended to have a hand-held trumpet held out in front. Before I knew it, I was strutting up and down the aisles between tables, doing the appropriate actions and making the noises. The room exploded in hearty laughter. Unknowingly I was the centre of a bet.

"I can get him to strut up and down prank."

I saw bets being paid out.

With the part of the twelve-week course now behind us, the final weeks crept on. Like a breath of fresh air, the welcome arrival of Assistant Divisional Officer Stanley Gudgeon took place. Working partly for the Home Office, he was our Brigade's Civil Defence Instructor. One of his duties was to recruit volunteers to man the dull green-painted appliances, the Green Goddesses.

He introduced us to the realms of the possible total annihilation by a foreign nuclear attack. A full week of comprehensive Civil Defence Training would come later, away from home at Moreton-in-Marsh, an old wartime airfield. Mr Gudgeon's manner and presentation, mixed with a dry sense of humour, was a welcome change from the never-ending dreary hours of classroom drudgery.

Flamboyant in attitude, he treated the possibility of the country being wiped out of existence very seriously, but with a touch of sarcasm. He believed the future for any still left would be bleak. Gas masks were issued to every fireman and we carried them obediently in their small brown canvas shoulder bags on all operational turnouts. We were left to ponder their effectiveness in the case of a holocaust.

His lecture was followed by half-day drill, using a couple of the Green Goddess pumps. I looked for the one I had left with damage to the front wing but could not find it.

Organised at a nearby Home Office site in old derelict houses, we practised searching, rescuing casualties and removing them from a possible future nuclear bomb attack. This drill provided realism at long last.

The final two weeks at training school arrived. Every single hour was now counted with glee.

Carrying down, the fireman's rescue lift had initially been attempted from a ladder pitched up to the first floor. By our final weeks, using a sixty-foot wheeled escape ladder, we reached the fourth floor, a height of forty feet. Everybody had to go through the ordeal of carrying a colleague down from the drill tower using the fully extended escape ladder. Then we climbed the ladder again before being slung over our partner's shoulder and jostled and bounced back down to the ground.

Hook-ladder drills also got ever higher. Serious doubts existed over the very existence of this ladder in the Fire Service and attempts to remove it from operational appliances followed after serious accidents were reported. But I found hook-ladders satisfying to climb even if they were not considered practical. In stages we all scaled the ninety-foot tower single-handed, carrying the hook-ladder from floor to floor.

Breathing apparatus drills too became more intensive. Taking long walks round the school tested the amount of time during which they could be used. For testing endurance in heat and smoke, an old brick-built chamber was filled with burning steel braziers manufactured from old oil drums and was fuelled by old tyres, wood and other rubbish, all of which were soaked in paraffin and set alight. We crawled round and round in the increasing temperatures and moved wooden logs from one end to the other. Pushed to extreme limits, the cooling properties of the calcium chloride became useless and our bodies and the contents of our lungs reached a critical temperature.

In these conditions the Proto breathing apparatus reached its working limitations. The rubber mouth insert was glued to the gums, our goggles pressed hard around the eyes, and the nose clips became welded to our nostrils.

As our training course reached the Friday of the penultimate week, we sat our final written exam. My fingers ached with the constant use of a pencil. Not since my secondary school days had I suffered so much; my index finger even showed signs of bruising.

When the last page of questions was almost completed, Assistant Divisional Officer Grayling entered and walked slowly to the front of the lecture room. He approached Sub Officer Hussar who was the invigilator. We stopped writing and looked up from our answer papers.

Mr Grayling spoke in a whisper. He walked slowly down the spaces between the desks.   Every one hesitated holding their breath. Stopping in front of my desk he bent low and quietly asked me to come to his office. The room hummed.

With my brain in overdrive I put down my pencil and pushed my chair back slowly. The wooden chair legs scraped on the floor, disrupting the silence. As I turned slowly to the door I could see Mr Grayling waiting patiently, his face full of concern. I tried a quick smile but there was no response. This must be the end of my career, I thought. Was it execution time? Every misdemeanour I had committed during my weeks at training school raced through my brain.

I followed exactly two paces behind Mr. Grayling, across the drill ground. Not a word was said. After the long walk to his room I entered after him and slowly closed the door.

"Sit down Michael," he said in a soft and kind voice. He was using my Christian name. Not an executioner's attitude I thought.

In the far corner of the room stood a uniformed policeman, staring out of the window. He turned to face me, his helmet tucked under his arm.

"I have some bad news for you," he said, "some bad news about your mother."

Mother. Mother. Training School and Mother. I searched to try and understand the connection.

"Your mother has been involved in an accident." His sentence was short.

"She has been knocked down by a bread van. I am sorry to have to tell you," he paused for a moment, "she was dead on arrival at the hospital!"

Mother. Not possible, I thought.

In a daze the policeman in his car took me to the hospital. The entire journey was made in silence.

Ushered into a cubicle at the hospital, I was shown a trolley on which was a body covered in a white and spotless sheet. A nurse stood at one end of the trolley. It wasn't my mother, surely. The nurse slowly pulled back the sheet; the policeman opened his notebook. I looked at the face and then at the blue-grey painted wall. I nodded. The policeman noted the time on his wrist-watch and scribbled something in his notebook.

I looked again.

Mother looked so serene. Her face was peaceful. Gone were the tight crease marks that had once lined her forehead. Her lips were a smooth deep blue.

I had never experienced death at such close quarters.

Divisional Officer Mullet, one of our senior officers, was waiting outside to take me home. I sat in his red Hillman estate car, stunned. I was glazed and blank during the journey home.

"Is this your house?" He interrupted my nightmare.

Two men stood on the pavement knocking on our door. I recognised one of the men. He was the regular rent collector; a small pathetic weasel of a man and at his side, looming high above him was a solid thickset hunk of a man. I dragged myself out of the car and stood in front of them.

"I want you out of this house," whimpered the small weasel.

"You're not living here on your own. Your rent finishes in two weeks, be out by then." Bad news travels fast, I thought.

Divisional Officer Mullet climbed out of his estate car, fastening his belt buckle and placing his uniform cap on his head. He glowered at the two. The weasel cowered behind his minder.

"Two weeks." His words drifted off. He scuttled off down the street, his bodyguard at his side.

Inside, the house felt cold. The dining table was laid with just one place set for my evening meal. It must have been the last thing Mother did. Divisional Officer Mullet produced a fresh pot of tea from our scullery.

He talked to me and tried to be reassuring. It was a wasted effort. After a while he gave up and left, telling me to let him know if I needed help.

Saturday and Sunday passed in a dream. I tried the contents of a bottle of kirsch I found in the sideboard but it gave me no feeling of relief.

One week was left to do at Training School, and it provided a welcome relief to my sadness and anger. Mother, my mind churned over and over, was only forty-four years old.

The final day at long last arrived and on Friday we had our passing out parade. For this special parade a series of demonstration drills which we had rehearsed was planned. They were to be performed in front of an audience of Chief Officers from all the other Brigades, and the families and friends of the passing out recruits were all invited, to make the event special.

Two items on the agenda were a live rescue from the drill-tower with a carry-down using the sixty-foot escape, and a demonstration using the hook-ladder. I found, to my surprise, that I was to perform the hook-ladder demonstration.

The drill tower was to be scaled from the ground to the top floor. I lifted the ladder and placed the hook on each window-sill and then climbed up and up.

At the sixth floor, sixty feet high, the hook-ladder dangled from its steel hook. Going into the building over the horns meant first gripping the two strings of the ladder that protruded from the top of the tower, like two stubby thumbs and then climbing up the ladder until both feet were between the hands. Then I stepped onto the top of the tower.

Mother would have been proud.

A Chief Officer from another Fire Brigade gave a complimentary speech and we were dismissed. He left us feeling a sense of achievement.

My twelve weeks' basic training was completed at long last. Although there was a great deal of trivialization and an endless obsession for cleaning, there were also one or two useful highlights. The practical experience I had gained from working alongside actual firemen on a busy Station made me look forward to the next hurdle, passing my two years' probationary period.

Returning to a home full of blackness and sorrow I felt at odds with a cruel world. I still had to find somewhere to live. But my panic lessened; the pressure was too great to bother with mere panic.

I took another helping of kirsch, but again alcohol did not help my depression.

The next day I awoke in a daze, hearing someone banging on the outside door. I pulled the curtains back to reveal bright daylight. It was mid-Saturday. Unlocking and opening the door I found Barry Bleck and two other Firemen. Across the street I saw a red Fire Brigade van. Barry threw me a newspaper parcel.

"Here, get some food down you," Barry said as I caught the parcel.

"We've come to rescue you."

I opened the parcel to find a late breakfast of fish and chips. I consumed the fish and chips straight from the newspaper, only now realising how hungry I was. My three friends bustled about the house and packed three tea chests with the contents of all the drawers in the house, the pots and pans from the scullery, the crockery from the sideboard. They helped me to parcel up all the clothes and bedding which were stored in the landlord's wardrobe into two old battered suitcases. Our two old beds were dismantled and everything was loaded in the Brigade van.

All my worldly possessions were in a single van. Like a helpless child I was pushed about. When the van was loaded, we set off. Barry Bleck told me that wheels had turned to get me some alternative accommodation. Eventually the wheels stopped turning; someone knew someone else who knew of an empty flat above a green grocer's shop. We set off. The van wheels, too, were turning to rescue me.

We struggled through a shop packed with green vegetables, up a tight winding staircase to two small rooms and a partly fitted kitchenette with the two beds and the tea chests. All my possessions stood at last in a heap on the floor.

Barry produced a crate of ale and we proceeded to christen my new home well and truly.

Chapter 7

My new black leather helmet, pristine and brand new, nestled like a roosting raven on a sheet of pink blotting paper.

"Your school report's not good Michael," Station Officer Finnan said. He pushed my helmet slowly forward.

"I'm sorry about your mother," he added in his northern accent, as my helmet reached the edge of the pink paper.

"But I'm pleased to hear you have somewhere else to live."

Kind man I thought.

But immediately he changed his tone of voice.

"You have only just reached the pass mark at training-school. The Chief expects all his recruits to be in the top ten." He stood up, turned away and faced a small cracked mirror suspended from a nail on the wall.

"He'll want to see you."

He produced a steel comb from his uniform pocket, peered into the mirror and combed his hair. He arranged the centre parting with precise accuracy. I collected my new helmet and grovelled out.

Outside the Station Officer's office, I tried my helmet for size. Made from compressed leather, it rested heavy on my head. My other helmet, forty or so years old, now went back to Stores to be re-issued to another raw recruit. With the smell of new leather lingering in my nose I pranced about proudly, brandishing my new headgear.

While I was enduring the three months away at training school, White Watch had gained another recruit, Malcolm

Cackerel. His face was dotted with small red spots, and three pink plasters on his neck covered large bulging boils.

Malcolm greeted me in a lilting Irish accent.

"How difficult is Training School?" He asked.

"It's physically demanding and we were always hungry," I replied with the satisfaction of someone who had completed the course.

The food provided at Training School barely bridged the energy gap caused by the amount of exercise we took. Constantly on the move, I was forever hungry. The large stodgy dinner we consumed midday and a second dinner at home at teatime was still insufficient to replenish all the energy I had used.

"If you're not fit at the beginning, you will be at the end," I told him with glee.

A new boy on White Watch would ease the pressure on me,

Complete with my new helmet, I felt pleased and proud to rejoin my watch. Received by my colleagues, who reserved judgement about me, I quickly found that all the techniques I had learned in Training School, drilling by numbers, marching, and formulas for working out quantities of water belonged in the class room.

Wearing my helmet, I strutted about the Station. But the bells sounded interrupting my performance.

'Job Out! House fire, number seventeen Dart Terrace, off Scar Road'.

I grabbed the rest of my uniform tunic, fire-boots, and leather belt and with my axe in my arms; I barged through the two swing doors leading from the muster-room into the engine house.

I ran around the back of Pump One, dodging the other firemen converging in answer to the call out. Around the Pump Escape I gripped one of the two large carriage wheels as I ran past. The wheel spun freely. I opened the offside rear cab door and climbed inside the rear cab.

The engine house doors banged open. The engine started. Pump Escape followed Pump One out in front of the Station. We raced away. It was mid-morning on a Monday and the tarmac roads were black with fine drizzle. Leading Fireman Henry Carp, the officer in charge sat on the left of our driver, Fireman Trevor Tailor. Tailor revved the engine and changed into a higher gear.

The newly promoted Leading Fireman Henry Carp had joined White Watch from Stour Crescent Fire Station, one of the four outer sub-stations of Torridge City, while I attended training school. Although he was only twenty-six years of age, Henry had attained the rank of Leading Fireman only four years after joining the Service. Breaking the normal eight- or nine-years' service others needed before their first promotion. His father was our Assistant Chief, and no doubt this had some bearing on his rapid ascent.

A younger version of his father, tall and thin with the same long thin face, Henry displayed the confidence and assured manner that came with knowing someone on high.

Pump One in front of us negotiated the main road traffic easily and disappeared from view. Pump Escape stopped suddenly to avoid a car whose driver ignored our wailing siren. We lost our momentum but soon picked up speed again and chased after Pump One. On the roof of the cab above us, the silver bell clanged and the chrome siren wailed, its note going up and down.

By the time we turned into Scar Road with its maze of terraced property and cobbled streets fanning off in all directions, there was no sign of Pump One.

"All the Darts are further along this road," Leading Fireman Carp said.

"Dart Mount, Dart Place," driver Trevor shouted, reading the small black and white name plates high on the red bricked house walls.

"These small cast iron name plates were not designed for easy reading," Trevor observed, as he stroked his crop of fair hair with his right hand. His left hand still steered the appliance.

"Dart Terrace!" Screamed Fireman Peter Margot, our fourth crew-member, wiping away steam from the cab window. Our Pump Escape shuddered to a stop as Trevor braked suddenly on the damp road. He yanked the steering wheel to the left and we turned into Dart Terrace.

A big buxom woman dressed in a full-length blue-flowered-pinafore dress, stood in the middle of the road. She was gripping a tiny girl by the hand; her other arm was folded tight against her chest. She hobbled towards us, dragging the little girl with her.

The small girl's face was dirty and rivulets of clean skin descended from her eye sockets where tears had flowed. Blood oozed from the folded woman's arm.

"Round the back, round the back," she screamed at us. As she moved her damaged arm, drops of blood flew into the air before landing onto the wet cobbles.

"Peter?" Leading Fireman Carp shouted from the front cab of the, "get the first aid box. Look after this woman." His words were brief.

Grabbing the black first aid box, Peter Margot leaped from our slowly moving appliance.

"Here luv, I'll see to you." Peter's voice tailed off as the appliance moved off, his door still open. It slammed shut as Trevor crunched the gear; the appliance jumped forward.

There was a small narrow alleyway at the rear of Dart Terrace. We saw smoke drifting from a downstairs window nine houses down. Pump Escape crept slowly with only inches to spare down the alleyway towards the smoke.

Crammed in the narrow back street opposite the smoking window, our cab doors would not open fully. Dressed in my uniform, with new helmet, my tunic, and my leather boots, I squeezed through the narrow gap, which the street allowed. My axe and belt-line, a small personal rope twelve-feet in length, which was rolled up neat and tidy, caught on the inside door handle of the appliance. However, by undoing the large shiny buckle on my belt I managed to untangle the mess and get out, leaving my belt line flapping and dragging behind me.

Leading Fireman Carp climbed out of his cab window dropped onto the cobbled alleyway and ran around the front of the appliance to the high gate of the burning house.

"Hose-reel!" he shouted.

There was barely sufficient room at the side of the appliance. I reached up and grabbed the end of the hose-reel and pulled on the end holding the hose-reel nozzle. The red tubing unwound slowly from its drum.

Trevor squeezed down the side of the Pump Escape and managed to organise the pump's controls, which were situated down the offside. The engine raced now that the hose-reel pump was engaged. I tested the water supply from the hose-reel nozzle. Water spurted out in a spray and I threw the nozzle and hose-reel over the garden wall and climbed up the side of the appliance.

Dropping down into the back yard of the house I stood alongside Leading Fireman Henry Carp. We were immediately showered with objects flying from the window.

A white enamel bowl crashed down near our feet on the cobbles. Chips of enamel flew off it in all directions as it bounced several times on the hard ground. Plates, bottles, pans followed. Objects rained down upon us from the broken window. Dodging these we reached the rear doorstep and pushed hard on the door. Henry entered first, forcing the door wider open. I dragged more hose from the appliance until it curled in loops on the doorstep. I followed Henry into the room, squeezing through a narrow gap and clambering over a broken chair.

In the far corner of the kitchen, at the side of a white pot sink, a partly clothed man stood. Dressed only in a pair of trousers, he was throwing everything he could reach out of the window. At his elbows, the curtains merrily blazed away.

Grey smoke drifted up and out of the broken window. Perhaps he was saving as much as possible, I thought.

Not fully understanding the picture I sprayed water on the burning curtains. Nothing else appeared to be burning.

The man was furious. Ranting and raving, he turned on Carp, shouting abuse at the top of his voice. His piercing voice turned the air blue. We stood mesmerised, not knowing the full situation. With a pair of braces over his bare shoulders and his fly gaping open he picked up a large pop bottle from the wooden draining board and swung the bottle crazily against the wall. The pop bottle would not break so he swung even harder. The walls cowered, but fortunately for us the screw top on the bottle remained firm and tight. Again, he hit the wall but still the bottle would not break. Undeterred he swung the complete bottle menacingly in front of Henry. His verbal abuse grew louder.

In a brave attempt to calm things down Henry tried saying words of comfort. The man turned, threw the bottle on the floor and stormed off towards the cellar door. He was still screaming obscenities at us.

We dragged the curtains onto the kitchen floor. I rolled them into a bundle carried them outside, and dropped them onto the cobbled back yard. They were still steaming.

The fire had not done much damage except to the curtains but the kitchen was devastated. The table and chairs were smashed and bits of food decorated the walls. Broken pots and pans littered the room.

Peter Margot joined us. Panting, he reported the tiny girl had taken a severe beating from this man. Her Mother, attempting to protect her child, had stopped a flying carving knife with her arm.

"They are safe in a neighbour's house," Peter gasped.

"The ambulance's coming," he added, between breaths.

Eventually Pump One and Station Officer Finnan arrived. Scar Road was over a mile long and they had approached from other end.

Noticing all the damage in the kitchen, Finnan looked puzzled.

"Bit of a nutter, gaffer!" Henry informed him. "He's disappeared into the cellar." On cue, strong thuds against the walls below us emphasised the man's presence. The house shook.

"Better get the police to sort things out," our Station Officer suggested in his Scottish accent.

The ambulance arrived and the mother and child were despatched to hospital. The fire was a result of domestic upheaval and although when we arrived, Dart Terrace had been completely empty of anyone but the mother and child, neighbours now suddenly appeared from all directions, offering belated advice. They stood in small groups, huddled together in the back alleyway.

We replaced our equipment on the appliance and made ready to return to the Station.

A police car arrived and parked behind the Pump Escape. A diminutive detective dressed in a grey full-length raincoat, climbed out from the car and squeezing past our Pump Escape and across the back yard he came into the kitchen. He was small in size but huge in confidence.

"Where's chummy?" He asked. We told him.

Making his way to the top of the cellar steps he peered down into the darkness. The madman, who was waiting at the bottom of the stairs, flared up again. The house shook as a big heavy iron bar, he must have found, crashed against the cellar walls.

"I need a lamp and a rope," detective stated.

Henry gave him one of our big heavy hand-held searchlights and I removed the line from my belt. Without hesitation the detective grabbed them and disappeared down the stairs. The iron bar banged, and the noise rang out furiously as the bar rattled from side to side against the wall. But not for long. A loud gasp was quickly followed by a scuffle and then by total silence.

Moments later the detective came out from the cellar.

"He's all yours," he said addressing two-uniformed policeman, who had now appeared, with another plain-clothes policeman. The kitchen was now crowded with people.

"I'll leave it with you, Henry," Station Officer Finnan said.

"Michael?" He added, "Come back with me. The Chief wants to see you. Best bib and tucker," he added without a smile.

Collecting my shoes from the Pump Escape, I climbed aboard Pump One and joined Malcolm Cackerel. He sat on one of the damp bench seats.

He was wearing an old-fashioned fire-helmet similar to the one I had been given on joining. It was too small and sat perched high on his head. From under the large brim one of the plasters on his neck hung loose.

As we pulled away from the incident we witnessed two burly policemen man-handle the apparent madman out of the house and into a police car. Trussed up, with the belt I had provided, like a joint of rolled sirloin he was thrown unceremoniously into the back of the police car.

Malcolm chattered in his Irish accent all the way back to the Station. But the thoughts on my mind were about my visit to our dreaded Chief Officer. Malcolm's nattering did not help. Although he perhaps meant well, it was a relief to be able to rest my ears from his constant banter when Pump One finally reversed into the engine house.

"Chief rang down just before we turned out. He won't be pleased to be kept waiting," Station Officer Finnan said as he descended from appliance.

Borrowing a uniform from several members of the watch, and sporting a new cap, clean and pressed trousers and polished shoes I looked reasonably tidy. With trepidation I made the solitary walk from the locker room to the headquarters.

The administration block stood apart from the engine house but lay in the same direction as our canteen. I mounted the flight of stairs and went along the corridor and I nervously opened the entrance door leading into the headquarters. I noticed a strong smell of polished linoleum as I tapped timidly on Chief Bass's door.

"Come in," he boomed. Gingerly I opened the wide door and entered the room.

My instructions were to go in and salute. Chief likes to be saluted, I was told.

He sat behind his large desk like an overgrown walrus, and I walked up to the front of the desk.

As smartly as I could, I stood to attention and saluted.

"Is that the best you can do?" Chief growled.

"Get out and come in again."

I crept out, turned at the door and re-entered and saluted again.

"That's much better." The Chief glanced to his left where Assistant Chief Officer Carp smiled and nodded in approval.

"Now, Fairn, this school report says you acted the goat. Is this true?" The Chief was obviously not amused.

"Well, Sir," I attempted to reply.

"It's not good enough," he boomed, "you young lads think life's a bloody holiday camp! I've had words with Mr Carp and your Station Officer and they both say you perform well at fires. All my recruits are on a two-year probationary period. Get out. I don't want to see you in here again."

I beat a hasty retreat.

As I returned the uniform I had borrowed for the occasion to its rightful owners, White Watch immediately grilled me about my appearance in front of the Chief.

Not a popular man with the lower ranks, Chief Bass still possessed his followers. In the Fire Service for nearly thirty-four years, and past retirement age, he stayed on and seemed to have no intention of relinquishing his command. Those who wanted promotion treated him with apparent and obvious reverence and never uttered a word in opposition to what they knew to be his views.

I already understood that promotion was gained through fear, favour and a touch of nepotism. Never to upset the hierarchy and perhaps to win favour by carrying out trade work on the Stations (if you had been a skilled tradesman before joining the service) or having good family connections were the routes for advancement.

On Fire Stations, firemen collectively, unless they were the privileged tradesmen, were an embarrassment. Work-creating schemes, high in manual labour content, filled our days when we were not called out. But when they turned out to incidents firemen changed miraculously from being a nuisance to something essential and important. Once back on the Fire Station, however, we soon returned to the humdrum of station life.

The ranks of Leading Fireman and Sub Officer were the two first major steps on the ladder of promotion. Both ranks ate at different tables and never mixed with Firemen during station routine duty hours.

When men reached the rank of Station Officer, and higher, their shirts changed from our common blue to white. They all ate in the officer's mess, which was furnished with a carpet and small tables, adorned by white linen table-cloths. They were clearly a race apart.

Under this pyramid I was happy to live and work alongside very experienced firemen, many of who would never reach any chance of promotion.

As I settled down on the Station it was to these experienced firemen, at the bottom of the pile, I turned to for guidance.

Chapter 8

David Edgar Capelin now aged forty-five joined Torridge City Fire Brigade in 1947 after having achieved an exemplary war-record. It was whispered that he held a bravery award and now endured a damaged right hip as a result of his wartime exploits.

Fireman Capelin's silent unassuming manner attracted respect from everyone in the Fire Brigade. An ex-marine and a practical man, David showed an ability to turn his hand to anything mechanical. He was protected from having to do much heavy work and spent most of his time driving our Station's two special appliances, the Emergency Tender and the Turntable Ladder. David loved to provide advice to anyone willing to listen. He willingly shared the knowledge he had acquired, and took great pride in explaining how things worked.

As the number of appliances on the Fire Station grew over its eighty years, first from horse drawn steam fire engines to the first motorised petrol Model T Ford machine at the turn of the century and now to modern appliances, the Fire Station needed room to expand. A converted property at the rear now housed our Emergency Tender and a Home Office Green Goddess.

The Emergency Tender, a 1957 Commer pantechnicon crewed by two men, the driver and an officer in charge, carried a mass of equipment in addition to that carried on the bread-and-butter appliances, the fire fighting pumps. Acetylene cutting gear, vehicle bottle jacks in varying sizes, extra Proto oxygen breathing sets, oilskin coats, spanners, joinery tools, saws.

Minuteman, an automatic resuscitation apparatus was part of the Emergency Tender equipment. Perched on the roof were three heavy steel legs and a block and tackle for lifting.

The road engine also powered a steel cable winch and a 110 volts generator for power tools and for electric lighting. E.T. as it was colloquially known was designed and built to Torridge City Brigade's specifications and supported two rear sliding doors and a walk-through interior. David was inside and was leaning against the workbench for support as he slid open a drawer and selected a piece of equipment to demonstrate. He carefully unzipped a brown leather pouch and removed a set of compact hydraulic bolt cutters, which were intended to replace the heavy and cumbersome hand, operated bolt cutters we carried on the pumping appliances. The cutting jaws on this small model gradually closed as David pumped the flexible handle.

"But they're expensive," he commented, as he meticulously described the workings and strength tolerances of the cutter.

His enthusiasm never lessened as we went through locker after locker, drawer after drawer. Driving the Emergency Tender regularly, David experienced several serious incidents, road accidents and industrial injuries. He knew the feeling of pain and death, which he saw at close quarters.

Stories of a serious house fire spread through the brigade on the grapevine as we reported on the last of our three-night duties. Red watch, the day crew, discovered an elderly couple and removed them from their burnt-out bedroom. Complete descriptions of both bodies which were severely disfigured, were given.

I knew the Fire Service dealt with such human tragedies, but I wondered how I would cope when it arrived.

David, with his wealth of experience, offered advice and acted as a willing mentor. Sitting in front of the coke fire on a high firm-backed solid chair in the long-room, our recreational area when on stand-down duties, the smoke from David's pipe fogged the room as he puffed away. I listened to his every word.

"Death and serious injuries, which we treat with respect, become someone else's problem once we have done our job," he began.

"To carry the burden back to the Station does no good. Emotions, like blood on the road, must be left at the scene," he tapped his pipe on the fireplace, "it's better to find other outlets to relieve the trauma." Tobacco fell onto the red-hot embers and sparkled for an instant, like a burning star.

I thought of my mother, of her funeral, its aftermath. I remembered my pain and feeling of great loss. Death was so definite, so final.

For some months Torridge City Council had been constructing new sewer pipes along Baysdale Road, a busy arterial road carrying traffic in and out of the city. Every two hundred yards large cavities in the road joined the underground tunnelling. These cavities, surrounded by upright railway sleepers and protected at night by red paraffin lamps, dotted the roadside looking like wooden fortresses.

Bells rang just after 2200 hours on one warm summer evening. Message was 'Pump One and Emergency Tender to Road Accident near some sewer works. Outside a shop at 583 Baysdale Road.'

The night air was warm and humid. I was a crew-member on Pump One; Station Officer Finnan was in charge. I collected my uniform and climbed aboard and joined the rest of the crew, Leading Fireman Henry Carp and Fireman Peter Margot.

Peter had been in the Fire Service for ten years. He was loud, outspoken and brash. His carefree attitude to life was attractive to all young Firemen.

Baysdale Road, like a spoke on a wheel, splayed out to the city boundary. I shuffled about on Pump One, which was opened back, concerned and nervous at the possibility of an approaching tragedy. The single lamp on front of the cab roof cast a thin beam of blue as it revolved in the warm night air.

From the bench seat, looking back along Baysdale Road, we strained in the gloom to see if our Emergency Tender followed.

House numbers usually started at the city centre with odd numbers on the left and even numbers on the right. We looked for a number on the passing buildings. Suddenly 155 jumped to 271.

Chasing past the dark wooden sewer fortresses and the reported scene of the accident, we slowed down. Suddenly the road was blocked by stationary traffic. The Pump swung to the opposite side of the road before it slowed down opposite an accident. Glass, bits of metal and a single car wheel were strewn all over the road the rear end of a car poked out from a shop window, its rear wheels on the pavement and the engine and bonnet were buried deep inside a fish shop window.

The fish shop proprietor stood in the doorway of his shop. His white coat was blood stained. Henry Carp and Peter Margot leaped from our open backed appliance and ran to answer his frantic waving before our Pump stopped. I followed.

The shopkeeper's arms flapped in the air. Agitated, he gabbled away as he tried to explain how the car had first collided with the sewer works and then ended up in his shop.

The fish shop looked more like a butcher's shop than a fish shop. Bright neon tubes flooded the gory sight with strong harsh light. There was blood on the floor and blood was spattered over the white tiled walls. A groaning body, partly in the car and partly through the windscreen, moved slightly on the car bonnet. The head was covered in blood and red streaks ran down its face. One eyelid opened and an eye pleaded for some relief.

"Over here Michael!" Peter Margot shouted as he climbed over the debris that filled the front of the shop. The shop lights, unaffected by the calamity, left no doubts about the horrific sight. I picked my way through broken glass and over torn metal and saw another body.

Henry Carp joined us as Peter's hand groped inquiringly.

A mixture of bells and sirens outside the shop indicated the arrival of our Emergency Tender and an ambulance. Feeling the body for any signs of life we found no pulse, no response, and no movement. I helped as we moved an arm gently. The head suddenly jerked forward towards me. I reached out to prevent further movement, stopping the head with my hands. Blood, which felt warm and sticky, oozed through my fingers. I was amazed. It had never occurred to me that someone else's blood would be warm.

I looked more closely. The left side of the face was completely missing and a mass of dark red greasy substance hung loose from a deep wound gouged into the skull.

"There's not a lot we can do," Leading Fireman Carp stood up, his hands dripping red. Three of us joined Finnan and David who were working on the body poking out of the windscreen. The driver's door forced open by a crowbar.

David, draped across the front wing of the car, ignored any pain from his hip and held the driver's body in his arms.

"Got his leg caught on the steering wheel," somebody said.

"Get the new compact bolt cutters," David told me.

I clambered over the wreckage and ran to the Emergency Tender. Opening the rear doors and racing down the Inside Passage, I collected the brown leather pouch from an inside drawer and ran back to the shop. I handed the cutters to our Station Officer who had managed to reach the trapped driver by going through the passenger door and crawling beneath the dashboard. He placed the jaws of the cutter over the rim of the steering wheel and pumped the handle. With two cuts the lower half of the steering wheel came away. Ever so slowly the trapped hips of the victim were eased upwards and came free. The body slid slowly through the missing windscreen and onto the bonnet. David and Peter tugged from the outside and from inside the car I helped Station Officer to keep both of the victim's legs free of the sharp remains of the steering wheel.

Willing hands took the weight of the body as it came agonizingly free from inside the car. It was a woman. We lifted her off the bonnet and placed her gently on a stretcher and then carried her towards the waiting ambulance. We wrapped the second occupant of the car in a salvage sheet and lifted him clear of the wreckage. Man-handled from the corner over the car bonnet, the body was awkward to lift in the confined space. As we straddled the broken fish-shop window one leg fell out of the bundle.

"He's got no shoes on!" David joked.

"Look, he's got holes in his socks!" His distraction served the purpose, taking our attention away from the horror.

With both casualties removed, the car, once a Vauxhall Cresta was made safe. The bonnet was prised open and the battery disconnected.

"Is the fish going to waste?" Peter Margot asked the fish shop man who had resumed his position behind the counter.

"Just about to throw it all away," he said.

"I love fried fish," Peter said. He had been a chef before he joined the Fire Service and liked his food.

"Anybody else fancy some fish?" He asked. Everyone else refused. Blood splattered all over the white tiles did nothing for our appetites. Undeterred, Peter tucked into a large piece of battered cod.

"It tastes grand," he announced discarding a chunk mauled by his dirty fingers.

"We've done our best. The world must go on. If anyone can't stand the blood, then they are in the wrong job," he muttered between mouthfuls of fish.

The shopkeeper, already shocked and now looking decidedly wan, was not pleased with our seeming nonchalance and air of unconcern, but I was to learn this warped sense of humour and trivialisation was not meant to be disrespectful.

It was a relief valve.

An outlet for our feelings.

Chapter 9

White Watch meandered along peacefully under a decent and capable leadership. We were like a sedate, untroubled river.

A Station Officer always had to be in charge of our Station and with Station Officer, Alec Finnan, on annual leave his temporary replacement, the recently promoted Andrew Charr arrived. There was a rumour circulating throughout the Brigade that connected Charr's promotion with his uncle's tailoring business and the dubious supply of officer's uniform. Charr stood glaring at us during morning parade and with his reputation, of being a perfectionist meant that our once tranquil river situation was suddenly threatened by an impending tidal-wave of destruction.

White Watch's normal contingent of officers comprised of Sub Officer Latchet (who was off the Station working as the Brigade's electrician) Sub Officer Gardon (off-duty, sick), Leading Fireman Loche (Brigade's joiner) and Leading Fireman Carp who was on annual leave. Thus, we were also short of junior officers.

To add more water to the rising river, Leading Fireman Bret joined us after his recent promotion. He stood alongside Station Officer Charr. With his fat grinning face, Barney Bret was the favourite nephew of Torridge City Chief Fire Officer, Mr Bass. Promoted from fireman to Leading Fireman, Bret came to us after his legendary brain operation. On the receipt of his chrome markings for his new rank this mythical operation was said to have implanted a phial containing wisdom and knowledge through a small hole drilled in the rear of his skull. Bret was another example of promotion through family connections.

"I'm in charge now," Station Officer Charr told us. Immaculately dressed in his new uniform, that fit his body like a handmade glove, his cloth peaked-cap, positioned with minute detail rested in perfect position, flat on his head. Manicured sideboards bristled with annoyance as his ears buckled slightly under the sides of his cap.

In his new Station Officer's uniform, he looked like a tailor's dummy. His shoes were polished to such a high degree they no longer looked black.

Standing on parade on a station that was old, well used and worn out, he looked dressed for a wedding at a scrap yard!

"There are going to be changes! Everyone is going to be smarter. And everyone is to do their job smartly," he screamed at us.

Standing next to Charr, Bret grinned smugly, expressing agreement. Bret continued to shout our names detailing our manning for the day. Then we were inspected. Their eyes were everywhere.

Station Officer Charr's intentions were to flood our sedate river situation sufficiently so that those would note his presence on high. From a once peaceful watch we were now under amber flood alert.

"After parade and proper appliance checks, properly, and I mean properly," his face reddened with the effort of emphasising his order, "everyone, before they change into their working overalls, will see me in my office," his voice rose in a threatening wail.

The older members of White Watch smiled wryly. One or two had already served with Andrew Charr during his twelve years' service and witnessed his privileged ascent through the ranks. He had received his mythical brain operation six years ago, and then promoted to a Leading Fireman then a Sub

Officer and now, prodigiously, a Station Officer in record time.

The outlook looked bleak. The river was still rising.

As we were still short of officers for each of our four appliances, I was detailed by Bret to ride as officer-in-charge on the Turntable Ladder for the day. Fireman Maurice Grundel, one of our senior firemen was the driver and operator.

We entered the engine house for our morning checks, as canteen man, Maurice immediately changed out of undress parade jacket into a full-length brown canteen coat. Maurice always wore a brown coat as canteen man. We sat in the crew cab of our 1955 Dennis F17 Metz Turntable Ladder contemplating the rising troubles.

"Both of you to the gaffer's office now!" Leading Fireman Bret suddenly shouted at us.

I dropped out of the crew cab and followed Maurice across the engine house, down the three steps into muster-room, and into the Station Officer's office.

Station Officer Charr, his new hat still perfectly aligned, his ears still protruding, sat waiting for us. A white handkerchief hung down from his left sleeve. His shirt cuffs showed equal margins of white obviously measured with extreme care. Leading Fireman Bret stood prancing at his master's side.

On the desk in front of them stood piles of assorted buttons. There were all kinds of buttons. There were chrome buttons in three different sizes each inscribed with the Torridge City coat of arms.

There were black leather buttons for use on our overalls, even a pile of miniature trouser-fly buttons. Every button sat stacked high on the sheet of pink blotting paper in the centre of the desk.

"I noticed on parade that you have two buttons missing from the cuffs on your undress jacket," he looked me straight in the eye. Like Scrooge bequeathing pennies, he counted out the appropriate number. I obediently picked up my two chrome buttons.

"Get them on for tomorrow morning," he ordered.

"Maurice Grundel. Your brown-overall coat needs two buttons," Station Officer Charr kept the same intimidating tone of voice. Maurice stood, mouth open.

Selecting two brown leather buttons, Station Officer Charr pushed them deliberately across the blotting paper. Maurice glowered defiantly.

"I'm not sewing any buttons on," Maurice challenged the Station Officer.

"Then you must ask your wife to do it for you." Charr's order was insistent.

"If you think my wife has nothing better to do than to sew buttons on," Maurice answered stubbornly, "then you're off your trolley!" I had never experienced such open defiance.

"Not only will you sew these two buttons on, in future since you are canteen man, I want my cup of tea in this office at every tea break," Charr said.

"I'll bring it, if you'll drink it. But just don't go far from a toilet!" volleyed Maurice, scattering the two buttons onto the floor as he left the room. I too retreated still grasping my two precious buttons gripped in the palm of my hand.

Leading Fireman Barney Bret picked up the two buttons Maurice had thrown down and scurried out chasing him. Bret's tubby face glowed red with anger obviously supporting Station Officer Charr.

"Buttons Charr and Balmy Bret," Maurice shouted to the rest of White Watch who were all lined up in the muster-room awaiting their button issue. The sentence was halted in mid-stream as the Station bells sounded. The battle was suspended as all eyes turned to the indicator board. It demanded a full turnout, with Pump One, Pump Escape and Turntable Ladder.

I grabbed fire-helmet fire-tunic and fire-boots from my peg and moved towards the engine house. As officer in charge of the Turntable Ladder I needed the piece of paper with the fire-message.

I ran through the swing doors to the engine house jostling with rest of our watch.

I glanced at the message Control had given me. It read: 'Fire, Reeve's Shop, Otter Square, off Parret Place City Centre'. I took the piece of paper and dashed to the Turntable Ladder.

Maurice in the cab revved the engine. The engine house doors already open the appliance edged slowly forward as I threw my fire-uniform up onto the nearside seat and climbed up over the front wheel into the cab. I slammed the cab door behind me. As we moved out across the narrow footpath before turning sharp left and heading down the street I reached down to remove both my shoes and slide on my fire-boots.

Maurice suddenly hit the brake pedal. The Turntable Ladder jolted to a sudden stop and I slid forward off my seat. A dark green staff car had suddenly appeared and shot across our front. The car mounted the pavement to avoid colliding with our front bumper.

"He'll cause an accident one of these days." Maurice cursed the luckless driver.

Assistant Chief Fire Officer Carp receiving the fire calls in his office regularly raced appliances to incidents. His staff car now sandwiched between the Turntable Ladder and the Pump Escape joined the queue as we all joined the main road traffic.

I continued to dress. Fire-helmet on first. Then my arms were forced into the tunic sleeves. As the appliance gained speed I pressed hard on the two floor switches which made the roof of the cab thunder above our heads as the bell clapper rattled inside the bell. The noise of the wailing siren rose higher and higher until it became a high-pitched scream.

My tunic at last fully buttoned, I thrust both feet into my leather boots before struggling to fasten the buckles on the thick Turntable Ladder belt. The large safety hook dangled loose from the belt on my left.

The early morning city traffic was busy and the streets congested. Pump One followed by Pump Escape and Assistant Chief's staff car cleared a path in front of us. We forced our way confidently through narrow gaps as the noise of our bells and sirens disrupted and stopped the normal flow of rush hour traffic. We raced towards Parret Place and Otter Square. When we arrived, the road was seized solid with traffic. Each appliance had to bounce across the pavement to avoid the congestion.

From a second-floor window in Otter Square a sliver of smoke drifted casually upwards. Underneath a window, in bold red letters, a sign read 'Reeves, Agricultural Merchants and Seed Suppliers.'

Pump One and Pump Escape pulled up in front of us.

"There's somebody in that window!" Assistant Chief Carp leaped out of his abandoned car and screamed at Maurice through the windscreen of our cab. My foot was still pressed firmly on the button and our siren continued to scream. Maurice decided our Turntable Ladder needed to be closer to the window. He manoeuvred slowly around the abandoned Pump Escape.

Still dressed in his brown coat, Maurice yanked the hand brake lever on, before leaping out of the cab. I ran to join him at the back of the appliance. Furiously he turned a big wooden handle. Four supporting jacks which were held back under tension from internal springs, suddenly escaped and spun down. All four hit the road surface with a clatter.

"Get on," Maurice shouted to me.

I climbed onto the rear platform and straddled my legs over the small wall on the sides of the ladder before stepping down to the rungs. Along the top section of the housed ladder I hopped to reach the head. I quickly fastened the hook on my belt to the securing point. Thrusting my left arm straight out, I indicated to Maurice that I was ready.

Maurice working from the roadside, elevated, trained and extended the ladder working the three hand controls in unison. Working the controls with speed and dexterity the ladder came off the appliance and turned as it extended. Clipped to the top of the ladder I was propelled up, out, and forwards. I looked up. An old man's face appeared for a moment through an open window. Grey and black smoke billowed out from the window. The face fell back inside.

The head of the ladder moved closer to the smoking window. I glanced down. Crews from Pump One and Pump Escape could be seen running inside the ground floor and dragging a hose-reel tubing after them.

The old man's face appeared again as the head of the ladder brushed against the window-sill. He still had his trilby hat on his head.

Maurice, even though he was a good sixty feet away, judged the distance exactly. I unclipped my belt and climbed up over the horns of the ladder. The sash window was partly open and I heaved the sliding wooden frame upward to gain more access. Smoke billowed out from the open window. Through the gap I dived in, head first. A voice moaned as I fell clumsily on top of the old man. I felt him wriggle underneath me. Grabbing the body, I man-handled him to the window.

Assistant Chief Carp following me up the ladder shut off any light from the outside as he covered the window.

"Over here laddie," he said.

I pushed the grey-haired old man towards the wall underneath the window. With an encouraging shove and a pull from our Assistant Chief, who was still outside on the top of the ladder, the old man clambered out. I followed him. With another fireman our Assistant Chief and the old man was guided slowly down the ladder.

The old man complete in his hat half-climbed half-fell into Maurice's waiting arms. Maurice bundled him onto a waiting stretcher. Two ambulance men wheeled him away.

Looking back at the window I saw that thick black smoke now covered the head of the ladder and spewed out. Maurice elevated the head of the ladder away and moved it from the smoke. Tiny fingers of flame muffled in black smoke suddenly exploded into a wall of fire. A sheet of flame shot out, licking and lashing the outside wall before curling over the facade of the shop.

I was then presented with a female coupling from the end of a dry delivery hose, fed to us from the Pump Escape. I climbed the ladder again.

Snapping the female coupling to a male coupling belonging to a length of hose already fitted on the ladder I climbed back to the top the ladder and waited. Almost immediately water shot out from the fitted outlet nozzle at the head of the Turntable Ladder. Water shot out straight through the open window and into the angry flames. Plumes of smoke cascaded out from the window as the fire in the room suffered under our onslaught of water.

Water from our Turntable Ladder nozzle soon subdued the angry flames. The jet of water from the ladder was then turned off. This allowed the crew, already inside, to have an easier ingress. Black smoke turned grey as water from the jet inside the building hit and finally killed a fire, which had been fuelled, by paper bags containing garden fertiliser. On further inspection we found, in an adjoining room at the rear of the premises, fifteen drums of sodium chlorate just waiting for the opportunity to join in the fun. We counted our blessings as the damping down operations commenced.

Two reporters pushed through the gathering crowds and approached our Assistant Chief Officer.

"We've pictures of the rescue," one of them said.

Our senior officers regarded all members of the press as loathsome creatures. The local journalist and his companion, who carried a large plate camera, were familiar faces at incidents throughout Torridge City. But they were always shunned and treat like undesirables.

"No comment." Assistant Chief Officer Carp said, addressing the man with a note pad and pencil. The Assistant Chief turned and walked away with Station Officer Charr running at his side.

With the Metz Turntable Ladder no longer required, Maurice rehoused it. The hundred-foot extension ladder was safely returned to the gallows, the four screw jacks were wound up and the appliance was made ready to return.

The truce created by the fire ended as soon as the appliances reversed into the engine house. As the engine house doors slammed shut, the outside world no longer existed.

Buttons Charr resumed his officious and demanding attitude.

"The appliances were not clean enough! You took far too long for your dinner break! And there are Station routines still to complete," he informed us.

Our moment of glory had gone. One minute we were chivalrous heroes rescuing a person in distress the next we were mopping floors and suffering again under the threat of further disturbances from our supposed flooding.

In the papers next morning, our dramatic rescue and fire was given front-page prominence. An action picture showed us rescuing the old man and walking him down our Turntable Ladder with Maurice operating the controls.

Were we heroes again we wondered?

A telephone call, from our Chief Officer, soon brought us down to earth.

"Who's the civilian operating our Turntable Ladder?" Chief wanted to know. The picture on the front page showed Maurice still dressed in his full-length canteen coat. In the black and white print, the dramatic photograph did look as if he was a passer-by wearing a raincoat. And, as Station Officer Charr was quick to point out, Maurice's coat was not fastened properly. And even worse his buttons were still missing.

Two long tours of duty eventually ended when our own Station Officer Finnan returned from his annual leave. Buttons as we had now christened him left us to inflict 'flood' damage elsewhere. Normality resumed.

Station Officer Andrew Charr never did get everybody to wear their full-button allocation. Nor did he get his cups of tea delivered personally. But he did not leave us empty-handed. Maurice surreptitiously, using a pipette, deposited drops of battery-acid on the threads of cotton behind every button on his brand-new uniform.

Until the next visit by Buttons Charr we were safe from flooding and a peaceful flow resumed.

Chapter 10

An excess of soot, the residue from domestic coal provided a bevy of chimney fires.

Twice a day during the working week thousands of families coughed into life as the coal-fuelled open fires in their house spewed out smog, which blanketed the City in a blue haze. These fires first burst into life in the morning and then repeated the process at teatime. Torridge City Fire Brigade attended well over five hundred chimney fires every year. They often disrupted our essential cleaning duties on the Station. Chimneys allowed the accumulated soot to choke their flues before catching fire. Our management and senior officers regarded this type of turnout as a nuisance. But for crews destined to be imprisoned on the Fire Station, these calls provided a welcome relief from station drudgery.

A call to a chimney fire, which dispatched our Pump Two to forty-three Colligan Terrace, came just after our 0900 hours Monday morning parade.

We approached the Colligans, an area not known for social graces, without making a sound. Brigade orders specified bell and siren was never to be used on such trivia as chimney fires or grass fires. Dressed in helmets, tunics and rubber-soled shoes (the smooth leather soles of our fire-boots were useless on slippery roofs) we sat on the rear bench seats for our Pump to arrive.

We could see thick white smoke, mixed with red sparks from burning soot in the distance. It spewed high into the grey October sky. Imitating a small volcano, a plume of smoke slowly descended and covered the surrounding streets in a thick acrid blanket. At the front door of number forty-three a young scruffy man stood. Sporting dirty trousers, which had been once white, and a brown jacket with the remains of food on both front lapels, he screamed at us as we stopped.

"You took your time," he yelled, every other word an obscenity.

Sub Officer Gardon, now back on duty from sick leave, did not reply but grimaced, keeping his feelings hidden. One of our most experienced and hardened Sub Officers; he rolled his eyes as we entered the house. I followed him, brushing close to the young man who was still in the doorway. A sweet smell filtered up my nostrils as we shuffled through the open front door and into the house. Still lashing us with his tongue, he followed us down the passage and into the front room.

The room reeked. Even taking shallow short sharp breaths produced a feeling of nausea. The room was packed tight with rubbish; partly eaten pieces of discarded food were sandwiched under a tower of plates, cups, and mugs all were stacked high on every available surface. On a partly hidden table in the centre of the room a mountain of cardboard boxes was piled high. Underneath them layers of filthy clothes were seen and muddled together in a messy pile. An old butcher's bike was propped upside down, its black greasy chain, broken and dangling, poking through the mess.

Every square inch of the floorboards was taken over by discarded pots, pans and bottles. Everywhere was filthy. In the hearth a fall of soot was piled high, like a black mountain.

As we walked further into the room through the maze of filth we placed our feet with great care. Our shoes squelched through damp partly solid objects beneath our feet. We did not dare to investigate closer.

Sub Officer Gardon looked at me but said nothing. He tilted his head as an indication that we should leave the room. His black fire-helmet with its two red bands, indicating his rank, rocked slightly. He rarely fastened the leather straps and they hung loose and dangled under his chin. The sulphurated air from the burning chimney outside felt kinder to our lungs than the atmosphere inside the house.

"Ladder up, hose-reel down the chimney," our Sub Officer instructed. He removed a silver-coloured tin box from his trouser pocket and proceeded to clear his vocal chords from the stench by taking a pinch of snuff. The rest of our crew, driver Fireman Trevor Tailor and Barry Bleck stood outside, away and free from the stench.

Removing it from the back of Pump Two, three of us carried the hundred and thirty pounds; thirty-five-foot double extension ladder to the side of the house. The heel or base of the ladder was held securely by Barry and Trevor as I pushed up on the two strings, or sides, until it stood upright and vertical. Barry came around the heel and pulled on the extension line. The head of the ladder extended, clearing the house guttering by three clear rungs.

Trevor, his uniform cap covering his short-cropped hair, pulled on the extension line to activate the pawls, a hinged securing device fitted on the top extension. Barry lowered the top extension until it came to rest on the pawls locking the two ladders together. Together we leant the ladder gently against the guttering. Being the youngest and therefore the obvious candidate, I collected the roof ladder, put it on my shoulder and began to climb.

The roof ladder was a piece of equipment designed to rest in the guttering and then to be laid across sloping roofs. Light in construction it provided us with easy access and prevented damage to the fragile slates.

Carrying the fourteen-foot roof ladder on my right shoulder I began climbing our main ladder. Glancing through a stained smashed window, I noticed that the bedroom contents were as awful as those were in the downstairs room.

When I arrived at the guttering, belching smoke from the offending chimney blew back down the roof and engulfed the top of the ladder. Almost blinded, I fed the roof ladder off my shoulder and slid it up on the tiled surface. Placing the heel, or base, in the guttering directly behind the strings of the extension ladder I waited for Barry to climb up behind me with the hose-reel. This process needed the weight of someone at the head of the thirty-five-foot ladder to prevent the roof ladder from slipping off the roof.

Barry gave me the end of the rubber hose-reel from the drum on the Pump curled in a loop. I transferred this loop onto my left shoulder and, pulling the hose-reel tubing, I clambered up on the roof. When I reached the ridge, I sat astride the apex and shuffled towards the chimneystack. Dirty grey smoke oozed freely from the chimney pot, shooting up into the sky as I stood alongside it.

Mortar crumbled in my hands as I held onto the stack. Suddenly the direction of the wind changed and I became engulfed in a thick fog of choking smoke. Coughing and with my eyes smarting I stood perfectly still until the fog cleared.

"We're not sheeting the inside. Just put water down the chimney," Barry relayed our Sub Officer's orders, which indicated that there was to be no protective sheet held over the fireplace.

When Sub Officer Gardon, a man of few words at the best of times, was annoyed his lips tightened to resemble steel pipes. With a face full of thunder, his eyes became ever more prominent and bulging as he stood in centre of the cobbled street looking up at me through the swirling fog.

Trevor, our driver, with the appliance pump now in gear and its engine ticking over, opened the water tank valve and allowed the eighty gallons of water carried in two on-board tanks into the water-pump. He increased the revs.

"Water on!" Trevor shouted up to me. He was holding his uniform cap in one hand. I shuffled up close to the stack, stood on my toes and just managed to push the hose-reel nozzle outlet down the chimney pot. Amidst all the hot choking smoke still jetting out, water shot out of the end of the hose-reel. The chimneypot hissed and crackled as the cold water went in.

We were using only a fraction of our eighty gallons of water, but the thick choking smoke soon gave way to white steam.

"Knock off and make up," the Sub Officer shouted up from below ending to the incident.

I went back along ridge tiles. My feet were the first things to go down the roof ladder as I gripped the strings of the extension ladder from the ground before I passed the hose-reel tubing to Barry. He grinned.

"The Sub's not too pleased with the occupier," Barry said as he took the tubing from me and climbed down to the road below. I lifted the roof ladder from the guttering and slotted it over my shoulder. With both ladders replaced the hose-reel wound back on its drum. Gardon fastened every tunic button for protection and looked up at the offending chimney pot. There were no signs of heat but only a whisper of gentle steam, which fluttered out in a single gossamer thread.

The Sub Officer once more bravely ventured into the filthy house. Trevor and I followed staying close. The front room did not look affected at all; the falling soot that had been disturbed by our water just blended in with all the rest of the accumulated filth.

"At least the rooms now covered in pure sterile soot," Trevor commented as he brushed his fingers through his short stubble of blonde hair.

"It's self-inflicted filth," he stated solemnly.

We returned to our Station and reversed the appliance into the engine house. We washed it, topped up the water tank and wiped the rubber hose-reel tubing clean, before we made a close examination for any foreign bodies, dead or alive, originating from the house at Colligan Terrace. The stench lingered for hours in our nostrils, and no amount of washing seemed to eradicate it.

Returning to Monday and our daily chores meant emptying and polishing the long-room, our main recreation room. We had a different floor to clean on each day of the week. By now, as I had completed nine months in the Fire Service, these daily rituals were imprinted as important and essential tasks.

As each of the three watches, Red, White and Blue, worked through the week, competition arose to achieve the highest shine on the red linoleum floor in the long-room. We polished the floor all afternoon. As we made the final buffing strokes across it using polishing rags under an old heavy table, alarm bells sounded for Pump Two. It was another chimney fire and we used the same appliance with the same crew as Sub Officer Gardon took the white piece of paper with our fire message from the Control Room staff. Another chimney fire this time at number 14, Girvan Place.

Once again, the chimney wagon, as Pump Two was sometimes known, pulled away from the engine house.

"That's all you're fit for," the rest of our crew shouted.

"Chimney fires are about your level. We'll stay behind for the proper fires," the guffaws echoed as we went down the street.

Girvan Street and Girvan Road were situated close to a large clothing factory. Rows and rows of neat back-to-back terrace houses criss-crossed acres of land. Clean tidy washing, draped on thin clotheslines, hung high across the streets. Large white bed sheets flapped merrily in the wind as we approached Girvan Place.

Hundreds of chimneys began their second life that day and threw out fresh smoke as people from the nearby clothing factories arrived home. Every chimney looked to be on fire as the fires were rekindled.

Outside number 14 Girvan Place a small petite woman stood anxiously. She was dressed in a spotlessly clean pale green cotton housecoat and was wringing her hands in obvious grief. She stepped back nervously and climbed up the three outside steps.

"I'm Mrs Thrasher, I'm very sorry to have to call you, but the fire in the grate is making an awful noise," she said, standing on her top step. Every edge of her three steps was scoured to a bright yellow with pumice stone.

"I've just this minute began to light the fire," she sobbed, "and my husband will be home soon," she added in a whisper.

Sub Officer Gardon, behaving in an entirely different way from the way he had done at the chimney fire earlier in the day, attempted to comfort her.

"Not to worry, Mrs Thrasher," he told her, "it's no problem. Let's have a look."

I followed him up the neat front steps and through her front door and into her living room. The house was neat and tidy. There were four chairs set around a square dining table; each chair was perfectly placed at each side. A brown chenille cloth was draped over the centre of the table. Neat folded corners, measured to the inch, were draped and reached the floor. A new brown carpet sat in the middle of the room, edged by polished linoleum. The floor shone brighter than the one back at our Station. The walls were covered in fresh wallpaper from which a large yellow and brown flower pattern shouted out.

"We've only just had the new fireplace fitted. The room's been completely decorated," Mrs Thrasher said. She held back a flood of tears.

"Have you had the old oven range removed?" Sub Officer Gardon asked.

"Yes," Mrs Thrasher answered quietly.

She produced a clean white lace handkerchief from her green housecoat and patted her nose. "My husband completely re-decorated the room and now it's all for nothing," she said, her voice trailing off and becoming barely a whisper.

We heard a noise, almost a groan, from behind the new fireplace as we stooped to listen.

"Have you any newspapers?" Sub Officer, asked.

Mrs Thrasher chased off into her scullery and immediately returned with a pile of old newspapers.

"I keep these for the fish and chip shop," she said, her hands shaking as she held them out.

We laid the sheets of paper carefully to form a pathway from the front door to the fireplace.

"Whoever fitted the new fireplace left parts of the old chimney stack still harbouring soot," Sub Officer went on to explain as I went outside. We placed our thirty five-foot ladder against the house and extended it to rest against the guttering.

All the houses in Girvan Place sprouted tall chimney pots, colloquially known as Long Toms. Some were more than six feet high and stood too high to be reached from the roof ridge tiles. To enable water to be poured down these pots we carried a chimney hose-reel adapter, a steel tube extension similar in shape to an up-turned umbrella handle. Fitted on the end of our hose-reel tubing, in place of the hose-reel nozzle, it was hooked over the high standing chimney pots.

I balanced on the ridge tiles, held the hose-reel adapter, and slotted the curved open end down the chimney pot.

The Sub Officer and Barry Tailor, working inside the room, first cleared the mantelpiece and placed a steel bucket in the hearth. Then they draped a chimney sheet, an old piece of canvas sheeting carried for this specific purpose, over the fireplace completely covering it.

Our Pump sent a quick burst of water through the red hose-reel tubing and up the thirty-five-foot ladder, over the roof and out of the hose-reel adapter. A spray of water shot down the high chimney pot. Standing beside it, I heard the water flushing down the chimney.

"And another," came the order.

The engine raced again as more water went down the chimney. If there were too little water the accumulated soot would continue to burn. Too much, and excess water flooded into the living room. On the third attempt trickles of cold black water dripped into the bucket, waiting in the hearth. I was told to come down from the roof and Trevor, his uniform cap still protecting his blonde short stubble, climbed up the ladder. This provided ballast and support and allowed me to climb down.

Replacing all the equipment, we went back inside the house. The amount of dust and damage from the flying soot was minimal. Mrs Thrasher was satisfied as Trevor comforted her.

"Sit down, luv," he said, "we'll make you a cup of tea." He walked into the scullery.

But Mrs Thrasher was horrified and insisted she would make the tea and quickly chased Trevor out of her domain.

Gardon first asked permission and then went upstairs to check the chimneystack. Using a lamp, he checked the roof space in the attic for traces of soot that might have escaped from damaged brickwork.

"You want to get the people who fitted the fireplace to have another look," he told Mrs Thrasher he returned. He hunted for his snuff-box.

"They've removed the old range but they've left crevices where soot can gather," he said.

He inhaled a potion of snuff and undid his tunic.

Mrs Thrasher carried her best china cups and saucers in on a tray and deposited them on the table. The handles were so delicate and small that our sooty fingers could hardly poke through their holes.

"Will I have to pay a fine?" Mrs Thrasher's parting words as we climbed aboard our appliance.

"No, luv," Trevor began hoping to comfort her. He stroked his fingers through his blonde hair and leaned out of the cab window.

"It's a myth, luv," he said, "in 1892, in Queen Victoria's reign, there was an Act of Parliament with a ten-shilling penalty for allowing chimneys to catch fire!" He rubbed his hair as he gave her this remarkable piece of knowledge.

"But not these days," he finished. His left hand reached over and put the gear lever into position as he smiled at Mrs Thrasher.

Barry and I sat on the outside bench on the appliance and waved goodbye.

Mrs Thrasher gently waved back at us until we disappeared from her view.

Chapter 11

Dark winter nights threatened, and the legalised arson of the annual bonfires brought our usual crop of street fires. For an added measure of lunacy, potassium nitrate became available at corner shops and allowed anyone to become a pyromaniac.

The yearly ritual of retrieving household rubbish which had been stored for months in back yards, in middens and on bits of land ready for the fifth of November celebrations created many dangerous fire scenarios. Boxes of fire-works, often stored by children at home, created an even better recipe for tragedy.

The build up to this yearly pageant began weeks before Guy Fawkes Night, and we began to turnout to several instances of prematurely lit bonfires. Autumn approached and as daylight hours diminished the Station bells sounded for a house fire in the Breamish area. This area was a district densely populated with back-to-back terrace houses, separated by once cobbled streets which had recently been covered in tar and gravel chippings. The Breamish area was within a mile of our Station and we soon arrived there.

Lines of washing were still draped high above the streets as we hurriedly looked for Breamish Grove. Washing hung, pulled up high from the ground on pulley systems. Riding on our two appliances, Pump One in front and Pump Escape behind, we crept underneath lines of clothes, all hanging lifeless and still.

At last we located Breamish Grove tucked away at the end of Breamish Terrace. The eight houses were some distance back and almost completely hidden.

A woman, a headscarf covering rows of curlers, stood on the pavement. She was breathless and agitated.

"Our young kid has set fire to his bed in the attic," she screamed.

"Hose-reel," Station Officer Finnan demanded his usual North of the border brogue more pronounced than usual. The order was unnecessary. Fireman Barry Bleck had already uncoupled the small leather securing straps from the hose-reel of Pump One; the red tubing peeled easily off the drum. He dashed for the house door, the hose-reel nozzle in one hand and a heavy hand-held searchlight in the other.

"Anyone inside?" Someone shouted.

"No!" came the reply.

"No. Simon has run off. His father'll kill him!"

From the rear cab of the Pump Escape I ran to join Barry as he entered the house. I followed him up the freshly scoured stone steps and through the open door. Barry, tall and wiry, barged confidently into the living room without hesitating for a second.

An uncovered single ceiling-lamp flickered through hazy smoke. It cast just sufficient light to show a brown painted door in the far corner of the small room. Was this the door to the upstairs rooms? The smoke over the tight twisting stairs thickened as we climbed to the first floor. We were in total darkness.

"The staircase to the attic is directly above this." Barry coughed as he spoke.

I followed him. The hose-reel tubing dragged behind and needed more and more effort as we twisted our way up the stairs. On hands and knees, we crawled through the smoke-filled first floor bedroom and across it to another door to which gave access to the attic stairs. The temperature rose as we shuffled up each wooden step and the smoke made breathing difficult. Barry, an established smoke eater who was reared on the tradition that the more smoke a man can take the better the Fireman, inched up the bare wooden stairs in front of me. His tall lanky frame was flat on the steps and the heels of his leather boots brushed against my face.

Every intake of breath brought sharp pains to my chest as I gasped for air. It was difficult to keep my eyes open, and I blinked constantly.

Staying close to the floor and so hiding from the dense smoke we groped our way upward like two slithering slugs. We clutched to breathe in the small pockets of clear air, which remained close to the floor, as we crawled up the stairs, which ended at the attic floor.

Barry shone his hand-held searchlight forwards through the swirling smoke. The beam of light was stopped dead by smoke. As the smoke swirled around through pockets of moving air, we could see a mattress glowing in front of us. Barry turned on our hose-reel nozzle and aimed the jet of water at the glow. A solid wall of smoke hit us. Breathing was impossible. For protection I chewed on my tunic sleeve as the damp wool filtered some of the acrid smoke. I bit harder and coughed. Barry continued to drench the bed. At first, he seemed unaffected by the choking conditions.

"Get downstairs," he grunted at last. The two of us crashed down the stairs, our boots scraping on the bare wood floor. From the first-floor bedroom, our lungs momentarily replenished with air, we made a final effort and climbed the narrow twisting stairs to the attic once again.

At the top of the stairs Barry made a dash for the attic window. In one quick movement he forced up the thick heavy glass window and opened it. It fell back on the slated roof with a thud. I joined him at the opened skylight. We took huge gulps of fresh air to fill our punished lungs. We jostled together, competing with the smoke escaping out into the night air. Refuelled, we continued to direct the spray of water onto the smouldering mattress.

"All right lads?" Station Officer Finnan shouted up the stairs as we turned off the jet.

"Come down for a rest," he coughed.

Outside we staggered as our boots crunched on the new gravel road chippings. The clean night air eased the sharp stabbing pains in my chest as the welcome supply of fresh oxygen-rich air flooded into my lungs.

"Get Stuart and Malcolm up here," the Station Officer shouted from inside the house to the rest of the crew, who were grouped round us on the road.

Stuart Cale, a fireman with nearly six years service, was not the keenest of men on the Watch. He was never a front man, and he was a born moaner; with two brown sad eyes he was our professional pessimist. From the tips of his black oily hair to the soles of his pale-grey woollen Fire Brigade socks, Stuart was always the Job's comforter on the Watch. He worked part time for the local undertakers and this was his ideal niche in life, fulfilling his insatiable appetite for disaster and providing a constant supply of morbidity.

Malcolm Cackerel, fresh from his twelve weeks at the Training School was still suffering from an outburst of boils. His neck sported a white bandage, which ended in a large reef knot tied under his chin.

Reluctantly Stuart, followed innocently by Malcolm, answered the Station Officer's command and entered the smoke-filled house.

Standing outside we listened to the mother of Simon, the young boy who slept in the attic. She told us why she had called us.

Simon, nine years old, had dashed home from school. Intrigued and fascinated by the box of fire-works, he tried lighting a thunder flash. In an instant the whole box burst into flames.

"Where's the young lad now?" Barry asked.

"Probably at his nanny's, up Breamish Mount," his mother said, "his father will sort him out," she added wiping her face with soot stained hand.

Refreshed by the fresh air outdoors we returned upstairs. The mattress was now scorched and burnt. We parcelled it up in one of our salvage sheets and together we carried the awkward parcel downstairs and dumped it near the outside toilets, where it added to the heap of bonfire material.

Enroute back to our Station we noticed that the Pump One crew in front of us was gesticulating about something on our cab roof. As we reversed into the engine house, Malcolm climbed up and retrieved a large pair of pink bloomers. It was obviously captured from someone's washing line, and we thought it prudent to say nothing; we deposited the bloomers in our rag cupboard.

The end of the Thursday day shift arrived at last. Thursdays meant a night out with the Watch. This was a weekly ritual when we were not working nights, and it was an occasion never to be missed. Dressed in my one and only suit, a quick sandwich having been forced down while I dressed, I took a short bus journey to the centre of Torridge and by seven o'clock I was downing my first pint of beer before anyone else had arrived.

'Bag a Granny night', as some senior members of the watch called Thursdays, always began in the Torridge City

Tavern. A couple of pints of beer and then en masse, we waltzed to the Wine Lodge for some white wine. For just ten shillings this intake of alcoholic courage was sufficient to make any girl unable to resist our advances. That was the theory, anyway.

"Where's Barry?" I asked. Barry, normally one of Thursday's regulars, was not present.

"He's not coming tonight," Trevor Tailor standing alongside Stuart Cale, full pint glasses in their hands.

"It's all that smoke he ate this afternoon," Stuart said, his car keys dangling from his hand. In spite of his miserable outlook to life, Stuart believed passionately that he was sent to Earth as a gift for every woman. His new Morris Traveller Estate was his door to success. He openly flaunted his car keys to impress any potential female in sight.

After a few drinks my world glowed. As the evening progressed we staggered onto the local dance hall, just in time to grab any willing female. But again, my success rate was zero. The night ended with me happy but single. I staggered down the steps of the last bus, trying to explain politely if a little incoherently to the conductor that passengers needed careful handling. The conductor just laughed. I jumped off the rear platform onto the pavement and staggered home to my flat.

The following day Barry Bleck was off work, sick. Patricia, his wife, came to the Station straight from the hospital. He was coughing blood when he got home from work. They called the doctor who ordered Barry to go to hospital.

"Told you Barry should have worn a breathing set," Stuart Cale said, "we carry breathing sets on appliances. Why don't we use them?" Stuart as usual talked the loudest. No one disagreed.

"The Proto-oxygen sets do take an age to put on properly, but our new Siebe Gorman sets are easy," he continued.

The Siebe Gorman compressed-air set weighed about thirty pounds and the air lasted for about thirty minutes. The apparatus consisted of a compressed air cylinder and a demand regulator valve in the facemask. Unlike our oxygen sets, the air-set did not have to be completely bled free of air when starting up. The starting procedure was simple in comparison with that of the oxygen sets.

Assistant Chief Carp suddenly appeared on the Station. With the news of a fireman in hospital his visit was expected. But he arrived with the excuse to tell us there were still not enough new recruits to implement the forty-eight-hour working week, regardless of demands from our Union. This new shift system, already agreed by other Brigades, provided an extra day or night off duty. The Fire Brigade Union had been negotiating for some time to achieve fewer hours in Torridge City Brigade but always the answer was no: there were not enough men.

"Bleck is going to be all right," the Assistant Chief said dodging any questions about when and if the new shift system would come into effect. He made a quick exit.

"Who wants to go and see Barry from work tonight?" Trevor Tailor asked.

"Count me in," David Capelin said.

Straight from work, the three of us piled into David's old Ford Zodiac and set off on our mission of mercy. We went to the hospital, but we were told that he had been discharged and was now at home. We piled back into David's car and set off again.

"Nice to see you all," Patricia, Barry's wife, greeted us, "he's in the front room. Go through."

Barry sat on the sofa. His face beamed. His red curly hair was groomed and tidy.

"Young Michael's here too!" Barry spotted me.

"Cup of tea, lads?" Patricia enquired.

"No thanks, Pat, we just called to see how Barry is," David answered.

"Michael, do you fancy doing my coal job?" Barry turned to me and asked. Always on the look out for more money, I accepted at once without thinking twice about it. Most men on the shift did extra work to provide additional money for a better life style. As I was still a probationer, such work was frowned upon but my take home pay barely covered my basic living expenses and any extra income would be welcome.

"My brother needs a mate when he's delivering coal," Barry said as he gave me the address of the coal-yard.

After my shift on Friday, Saturday and Sunday nights I arranged to meet Barry's brother, Gilbert, on the following Monday, a week before Bonfire night. The going rate was four shillings per hour, and with no one to know about any deductions this was more per hour than my Fire Brigade pay.

Meeting Gilbert for the first time I was startled to see that they looked identical. Same colour hair. Both tall and thin.

"This is Barnacle Bill; he's worth his weight in gold." Gilbert said, introducing a big heavy yellow Labrador. The dog took centre spot in the front cab of the coal lorry. Perched behind the gear lever, he looked out of the cab window and drooled as he watched the world outside. He displayed several lumps on both front legs. Gilbert explained

"The vet says the lumps can come off. But Bill's too old for operations," Gilbert said as we drove away.

Barnacle Bill knew somebody was talking about him. The dog looked at his master with his mouth open, his tongue out. He understood every word.

We first drove to a railway siding to bag four tons of loose coal into large waist high hessian sacks.

"Barnacle Bill stays in the cab," Gilbert said as we climbed down from the cab so that the empty lorry could be weighed. Then we drove off the weigh-bridge towards the railway trucks, stacked with mountains of coal.

"Hold the bags wide open but tuck your thumbs underneath out of the way of the shovel," Gilbert advised.

The large steel shovel scraped on the floor and pieces of coal flew into the bag without pausing. Gilbert lifted each bag when it was full on to a set of scales. There were two fifty-six-pound weights on one side, and each bag was adjusted with an odd piece of coal until it tipped and balanced one hundredweight exactly.

It was nearly mid-day before we had filled and stacked eighty-one bags on the back of the lorry. On the way out of the coal yard Barnacle Bill was allowed to run about. He was not in the cab for the out-going weighing and he was indeed worth his weight in coal!

As we arrived at our first customer I strained to carry a bag of coal on my back. The savage lumps of coal dug deep into my back. I thought it was easier to carry someone down a ladder than to have such an inert solid mass bearing down on a pair of unsteady ankles. No wonder Barry and his brother Gilbert were so strong!

In front of every terrace house in the Breamish area was a tiny grate at floor level. We first emptied the sacks onto the paving stones and then the loose coal was slotted by shovel into the cellars through the tiny grate.

"Do I know you?" A customer asked Gilbert as she paid her money.

"Were you in a fire-engine the other day? You came rushing along here and took a pair of my new pantaloons from my washing line," the old woman said as she put her change into a tiny purse.

"You went to our kid's house further down in Breamish Grove, didn't you?" Simon's Nan said. I suddenly remembered Simon's escape from the fire on our fire-call earlier.

"Not me, Misses," Gilbert replied.

I did not have the courage to explain that her bloomers were in our rag bin. I quickly joined Barnacle Bill in the lorry.

After a full day of bagging, carrying, and shovelling coal I was exhausted. I climbed into the cab after we had finished the final delivery and stroked Barnacle Bill with my dirty hand. I was filthy from head to toe and I ached all over. But I collected my hard-earned twenty-eight shillings. Night duty began on the fifth of November began, and we expected to be busy. The first call came, to an unlit bonfire under some electric power lines.

Sub Officer Kevin Gardon, in charge of Pump Two, rolled his eyes as Pump Two stopped alongside some waste ground. Slowly he dismounted and walked towards a policeman sitting astride his police motorcycle.

An unlit bonfire towered into the night sky between two overhead high pylons. Six heavy cables, draped between the pylons, could be seen in the dark sky.

We dismantled some of the large wooden crates and spread the material away from possible danger. Leaving the policeman to trace the culprits we returned to the Station and had just begun to clean the appliance when the bells went again. Breamish Place. A bonfire.

"That's where we were the other Thursday!" Fireman Stuart Cale said.

"That was the Grove," Sub Officer Gardon corrected.

"Breamish Place is the next street."

The dark night air was filled with the smell of bonfires as residents all over the City began their Guy Fawkes celebrations. We passed several fires. Groups of people were standing around and an odd rocket shot up, leaving a trail of sparks.

Turning into Breamish Place we were suddenly confronted with a whole road on fire. A molten river of burning liquid tar ran down to greet us. A bonfire at the far end of Breamish Place was well alight. Flames fanned by a good wind, showered sparks high into the sky.

"Get a line on," Sub Officer Gardon ordered meaning we should get water from a street hydrant.

"And keep the appliance well clear!"

He strolled up towards the bonfire.

"Who's in charge here?" He asked. Everybody looked unmoved; their eyes were uncommitted. The glow from the fire was reflected in their vacant faces.

"You can't have a bonfire here!" Gardon's eyes nearly popped out of their sockets. There was no response. Picking on one person, he asked his question again.

"We've always had a bonfire here, in this street, since I was a lad," the reply came.

"But the road now is covered with tarmac." Sub Officer Gardon appealed for reason.

Together with Stuart Cale we helped our driver, Trevor Tailor, to locate the nearest hydrant and ran out a line of delivery hose.

"Water on!" A solid jet of water from the open end of the delivery hose soon curtailed the stream of fire. The liquid river of molten tarmac froze solid and stopped dead. But the new road surface was now scarred and ruined.

"Fancy some pie and peas?" The old woman asked as we prepared to leave. I recognised the woman from when I had delivered her coal and tucked my head out of sight into the top of my open tunic.

"Simon, go get these firemen some food for your Nan," the bloomer-missing woman said.

Simon looked none the worse for his escapade earlier in the week. He ran off and brought each of us a basin containing a pork pie, covered with a lump of mushy peas and swimming in vinegar.

"Find another site for your bonfire next year," Sub Officer Gardon said. We stuffed our mouths with food and left. Until next year.

Chapter 12

There was no public transport on Christmas day. This meant walking to the Fire Station.

It was a mile-long walk through the empty, cold deserted streets, which gave the impression of a world on holiday. It seemed that only firemen worked during the festive season. As a bonus for receiving no extra payment for working on Bank Holidays, we were allowed to stand-down and the Station cleaning routines were deferred.

Living on my own, I welcomed the comradeship and the chance of being with others as well as the promise of a turkey dinner. I looked forward to being on duty.

Normally the senior officers made a point of visiting Fire Stations at Christmas, but the latest decision to delay our reduction in hours to a forty-eight-hour shift system caused problems. Many Fire Brigades nearby already worked fewer hours for the same pay, and our rumblings of discontent went on bubbling under the surface. Extra recruitment had still not reached the required levels, and so our Chief Officer and Fire Brigade Watch Committee refused to discuss the matter any further.

Christmas dinner, complete with all the trimmings, was to be ready by one o'clock. Maurice Grundel, the canteen man, wearing a fresh clean brown coat, complained in his usual droning fashion that he needed assistance to prepare the dinner.

I was volunteered for this with Malcolm Cackerel, another probationer. We were immediately detailed to the canteen where to prepare, cook and serve a full Christmas dinner for eighteen men seemed a formidable task.

The vegetables, bacon, sausages had all been dumped on the kitchen table. In the centre of the table an enormous turkey sat with its legs trussed, abandoned on a thick wooden chopping board. Acres of cold white skin covered the twenty-five-pound bird. Roads from its blue-blood veins spread round spikes of stubble.

Maurice disappeared, leaving just the two of us to attack this mountain of uncooked and unprepared food. I peeled my way through the heap of potatoes, using a knife that would have trouble slicing soft cheese. Eventually two large pans were filled with rocks of roughly hewn potatoes. They stood on the stove waiting to be boiled.

Maurice reappeared.

"There's more potato thrown away than for eating," he said, peering in the waste bin.

Malcolm meanwhile took charge of roasting the massive turkey, plastering its white skin in inches of lard. Then he slotted the bird into the oven.

"Where are the giblets?" Maurice asked.

"What giblets?" We asked.

The turkey, which was heating nicely, was immediately retrieved from the oven. Malcolm slid his hand inside the warm rear-end and retrieved a paper parcel containing a heart and pieces of liver.

"We'll need that for the gravy," Maurice said.

Unknown to us help was on the way. The ex-chef, Fireman Peter Margot was our saviour. Everyone but us knew Peter would be the master cook for the day. He had worked in the catering trade before joining Fire Brigade and when he arrived on the scene, he considered all our toils and troubles absolutely useless. The potatoes were not peeled properly, the Brussels were untidy, and the carrots not clean.

A white tea towel wrapped around his waist, Peter set about methodically redoing all our preparations. The potatoes were re-eyed, reshaped and sorted into four different pans for boiling. Each Brussels sprout was inspected, washed and manicured with his personal sharp knife to look neat and presentable. The carrots were given the same fastidious treatment; after being sliced diagonally they sat in their pan like works of art.

Now relegated to being mere assistants, we willingly carried out every order Peter gave us. He removed the turkey from its premature incarceration, scraped off our coating of grease, filled the inside with handfuls of stuffing, re-coated the skin with a layer of butter and herbs and placed the bird back in the oven. Malcolm's task for the rest of the morning was to nurse this twenty-five-pound monster into a golden roasted offering. He was still suffering from boils and two new plasters adorned his forehead as more ulcers sprouted. He guarded the large oven with his life all morning. His face glowed from the ensuing heat as he regularly opened the oven doors to baste our enormous bird.

Under the ever-watchful eyes of our Chef-cum-Firemen, dinner eventually arrived; complete with an aroma that tantalised every taste bud. The rest of our watch, who had already enjoyed a few pints of beer from the Station bar, waited like hungry vultures.

The officers on duty, Station Officer Finnan and our two Sub Officers, took it upon them to serve everybody's dinner as we all sat down. This was a Christmas ritual and a break from our normal procedure, at all other meal times there was a segregation policy. Officers always ate in the officers' mess, an adjoining room that was specifically for Station Officers and above. In the Station canteen there were tables used only by Sub Officers and Leading Firemen. As Firemen we normally sat on our own.

But this was Christmas and for this one mealtime the privileges of rank were relaxed.

Station Officer Finnan carved the huge roasted turkey, producing a stack of white meat. Meanwhile Sub Officer Gardon poured thick vegetable soup from a pot jug into our empty dishes as we sat, our spoons rattling on our tables.

The flat ten-inch plates were too small to accommodate the enormous dinner that followed the soup. Sub Officer

Latchet gingerly carried our heavy steaming plates from the kitchen to our tables. Thick slices of white turkey meat, its edges crispy brown, draped themselves over the sides of our plates. Mountains of roast potatoes, green vegetables, sausages, creamed potato croquettes, bacon, bread sauce and finally, on the slices of turkey, a puddle of rich thick gravy completed the meal.

Just to be Peter's assistant felt good. Showers of gratitude and praise greeted us from stuffed mouths. The dinners slowly disappeared, eaten with enormous relish. The room fell silent. The scrape of knifes and forks on plates were the only sound to disturb the silence.

The noise from the tiny bell high on the canteen wall tinkled, rudely interrupting our dinner. Chairs scrubbed across the concrete floor as we groaned with disbelief.

We dropped our knives and forks, left our dinners and took off on the long run to the engine house. Maurice Grundel, drumstick in one hand, was the last to leave.

The control staff ladies also worked on Christmas Day. She stood waiting outside the Control Room door with a strand of silver tinsel in her hair.

"The alarm panel showing a fire at Merling's Store, Brett Street City Centre," she said as the piece of tinsel slipped over one eye.

Giving out three hand-written messages, one for each appliance - Pump One, Pump Escape and the Turntable Ladder - she stood, smiled and watched as we all climbed aboard our appliances.

In my tunic, my boots in my arms, my helmet plonked on my head, I climbed onto Pump One.

Outside the streets were completely deserted. Unlit Christmas lights were dead, draped high across the street on thick cables. In the daylight hours they lost their touch of magic.

Our three appliances quickly arrived in Brett Street and pulled up alongside Merling's, a large city-centre shop, which sold everything from food to furniture. It stood deserted for the holidays.

Station Officer Finnan climbed down from his front cab and looked through the front windows. Holding his white fire-helmet casually in his right hand, he stooped and stared through the plate glass window.

Sub Officer Latchet, in charge of Pump Escape, dismounted and joined the Station Officer on the pavement. A small red-faced man wearing an old grey raincoat puffed his way out of the store through a small side door. The remains of a thick cigar jutted out from his mouth.

"I smelled smoke," he said.

"Who are you?" Station Officer Finnan asked.

"Caretaker," he answered taking a breath around the sides of the thick cigar.

Someone else worked on a Christmas Day. Good I thought.

"When I called in to check the building," he began, "I noticed a smell of smoke." He sucked in air and let out a mouthful of smoke without removing the cigar. His words mingled with the exhaled smoke. His face was obscured behind a blue cloud.

"I broke an alarm glass. I hope I did the right thing?" he coughed.

We followed him through a door into the store. A series of coloured bulbs pulsated silently from electric bulb holders high on the ceiling. Their coloured display flickered and danced on the dark walls of the empty store. The caretaker breaking the glass fire alarm activated a direct telephone link to our Brigade and set off the fire alarm in our Control Room.

We searched the ground floor but found no trace of smoke.

We located the point where the glass was broken. Station Officer Finnan, using a piece of cardboard, temporally repaired it and Sub Officer Latchet re-set the alarm system at the front entrance. The pulsating coloured lights on the ceiling went out.

"There was smoke," the caretaker insisted, "it was near the shop window."

We looked again and sniffed the front display windows. There was no trace of any smoke, not even a whiff.

"We'll take a look outside," our Station Officer told the caretaker, "it's more likely smoke from his Christmas cigar," he muttered under his breath as we all went outside.

Merling's shop was jammed between adjoining stores and this meant we had to walk around the complete complex to reach rear of the premises.

"There should be an alley-way leading to Moyle Yard and the loading bay at the back," Maurice Grundel told us from the open cab window.

"Can anyone smell anything?" Someone asked.

"It'll be my Christmas pudding that's burning!" Maurice shouted. He was still sporting his brown coat. He took a bite from his turkey leg as he crunched Pump One into gear. We climbed on the rear running board as the appliance moved down Brett Street. The alleyway entrance to Moyle Yard from Brett Street was not wide enough to allow our Pump to enter. We dropped off the rear platform and, thinking more of our stomachs than of a false alarm, headed off to the rear of the store, walking through a narrow path to Moyle Yard.

Nothing. No smell. No sign of anything.

"Let's get back to the Station." Station Officer decided.

Three appliances returned as fast as they had come.

The crews of Pump Two and the Emergency Tender, who had remained on the Station, salvaged the deserted remains of our dinners. Marking each plate with our names on pieces of cardboard, they had placed them in a warm oven to await our return.

Locating our half-eaten dinners, we resumed eating I was just about to stuff a fork loaded with a piece of bacon, sausage and stuffing into my mouth, when the bells sounded again.

Fortesque Hotel, Moyle Yard.

A full turnout again, with Pump One, Pump Escape and Turntable Ladder.

Once again, we left our part eaten meals, this time for the Fortesque, a three-star, hundred-roomed city centre hotel which was fully staffed, even on Christmas Day. Access was at the rear of Merling's store. As we turned into Moyle Yard, the approach road was blocked by a couple of taxis and an ambulance.

More people who had to work at Christmas.

We ran the last few yards and entered front foyer of the hotel to find an anxious manager waiting.

"I didn't want to bother you on Christmas Day, but there's a smell of burning in the cellar," he said.

I followed Station Officer Finnan. We trooped down a flight of deep piled carpeted staircase, through a staff entrance, along a dark corridor and entered a wired-caged wine cellar. We looked and sniffed around. There was no trace of anything. The manager insisted there had been a smell and even a trace of blue smoke, but there was nothing and he apologised profusely all the way upstairs.

In the hotel foyer a group of his inebriated guests cheered the rest of our crew waiting outside. The ambulance departed, taking an expectant mother to Torridge City Maternity Hospital. Two taxis, crammed with the rest of her family, followed in hot pursuit. It was, they drunkenly shouted, a possible Christmas Day birth at the hospital.

More Christmas Day workers.

Once again, we were tucking into the remains.

Blanche Spurling, our faithful cook, had left us one of her famous Christmas puddings. Steaming all morning, the end result was a rich, solid lump of piping hot concentrated fruit, drenched with brandy. Each spoonful was covered in an avalanche of brandy butter sauce. The last mouthful took some forcing down. After consuming more than enough I felt and looked like the pudding heavy, rich and oozing with goodness.

The mountain of washing up was stacked high and filled every conceivable spare inch in the kitchen.

Peter Margot was indeed a good chef and his presentation and his food was excellent. But the number of plates, pots, pans and other crockery swamped the entire kitchen. A good hour elapsed before everything was finally washed and replaced. We all collapsed in a heap. But our rest was short lived. Bells sounded again. And again, the call was to Merling's Store, City Centre, Brett Street. Only Pump One, with the Station Officer was to attend this time.

I grabbed my fire-uniform and we left once again for Brett Street where we found exactly the same conditions. The caretaker again insisted he could smell fire. This time he did not break the glass of an alarm but rang nine-nine-nine. The cigar in his mouth looked no different. Still gripped tight between his lips, it stuck out like a thick stubby carrot.

Station Officer Finnan stood in the middle of Brett Street, his arms folded. His white helmet under his arm, his feet apart, he listened patiently to the caretaker. Again, we searched the building. But we still could find no sign of anything untoward.

We returned to the Station as daylight faded.

The appliances, even on Christmas Day, needed to be washed-down with soap and water and leathered dry for the night watch, which would take over. Even the floor of the engine house needed its obligatory mopping; we glossed it over with water. As all hands busied cleaning, the bells sounded for the fourth time.

"Brett Street near Merling's Store again. It's a call from the police!"

Torridge City Centre streets now sparkled with Christmas lights. The roads were still deserted as we sat outside on the bench seats on the back of Pump One; strings of lights dazzled above our heads. On the pavement outside Merling's Store a policeman and his sergeant were standing waiting for our arrival.

A hundred yards away from Merling's Store, the policeman on his Christmas Day beat found that a steel inspection lid set in the pavement was breathing out a whisper of smoke.

Using our crowbar, we lifted the lid and exposed underground electric lighting cables and found the problem. The extra power required for the festive illuminations had allowed a cable to overheat, causing the protective bitumen to melt and then to smoulder. Smoke percolating through pipes below ground had seeped into Merling's Store and eventually, through the ducting, underground into the cellar of the Fortesque Hotel. Using the appliance's radio, Station Officer Finnan requested the attendance of street lighting electricians.

Someone else was working during the festive season!

The electricians arrived and soon isolated the supply. Lines of Christmas lights went out all along Brett Street. But the City was now safe.

All the characters and place names in this book are fictitious
and any resemblance to actual persons and locations living or dead
are purely coincidental.

All 'Job Out' books are available via Amazon
Type me fairn in search facilities

Printed in Great Britain
by Amazon

77562425R00072